IMAGES
of America

LOS ANGELES'S
LITTLE ITALY

IMAGES
of America

LOS ANGELES'S
LITTLE ITALY

Mariann Gatto

ARCADIA
PUBLISHING

Published by Arcadia Publishing
Charleston, South Carolina

Printed in the United States of America

Library of Congress Control Number: 2009926175

For all general information contact Arcadia Publishing at:
Telephone 843-853-2070
Fax 843-853-0044
E-mail sales@arcadiapublishing.com
For customer service and orders:
Toll-Free 1-888-313-2665

Visit us on the Internet at www.arcadiapublishing.com

This book is dedicated to my son Damian Gatto, the light of my life, who has been as much of a teacher to me as I to him, and to my father, Joseph Gatto, who taught me the importance of education. It is further dedicated to my nonna—Maria Antonia Cortese Gatto—whose sacrifices within this country inspire my work, and to my nonnu, Mercurio Ferdinando Gatto, who, at age 18, left his village, never to see his parents and brother again, not to see his sister until the final years of his life. May this publication inspire others to memorialize the struggles of the immigrant to achieve the American Dream.

CONTENTS

ACKNOWLEDGMENTS

I am grateful to the many people, organizations, and institutions that played an integral role in the creation of *Los Angeles's Little Italy*, including the historians whose work contributed to my understanding: Rosalind Giardina Crosby, William Deverell, Lawrence DiStasi, William Estrada, Michael J. Eula, Joseph Giovinco, Richard Griswold del Castillo, Olive Kirschner, Gloria Ricci Lothrop, Jerry Mangione, Ben Morreale, William McEuen, Ricardo Romo, George Sanchez, Kenneth Scambray, and Mark Wild.

I wish to thank my family, especially Damian Gatto, Joseph Gatto, and Dr. Nicole Gatto, and my steadfast friends Lauren Wayne and Anna Kunkin for their support throughout the years. I am especially grateful to Margaret Bryant for her counsel and Peter Espinoza for the changes he brought to my life. I would also like to acknowledge the individuals who encouraged me to write this history: Carol Jacques, Mark Martinez, Bill Rumble, Ronn Savala, Don Sloper, and Dr. Carol Srole.

This text would not have been possible without the Italian community who shared their stories, especially Josephine Mahoney, Sergio and Elsie Bracci, Carl Lo Cascio, Margaret and Louis Bisetti, the Claro family, Dr. William Fasoli, Mike Pagone, Mary DiMaio Wallace, Eda Tortomassi, Elda Maga Pilj, the Angiuli family, John Nese, the Perricone family, Mary Messarotti Oliver, Josephine Romano Lyden, the Costantini family, David and Juliette Aprato, Connie Costa Foster, Michael Martini, the D'Egidio family, Mario Trecco, Marsha Johnson, Gloria and George Carone, Robert Barbera, the Paggi family, Art Almeda, Al Vignolo, the Riboli family, Marisa Antonini, Anthony Valla, Lynn Slosson, Ben Piazza, Robert Arconti, Roy Fazzi, Bruce Festa, James Frida, James Griffin, and Linda Marcus.

I thank Los Angeles councilman Dennis P. Zine for his generous financial support of my research and am grateful to the research scholars who assisted: Caitlin Clerkin, Valentina Licitra, and Janina Maniol.

The staff and resources of the following organizations and institutions proved invaluable: the Historic Italian Hall Foundation, Anaheim Public Library, Archdiocese of Los Angeles, Archivo Magòn, Bancroft Library, Buena Park Historical Society, El Pueblo de Los Angeles Historical Monument, Federated Italo Americans, Honnold/Mudd Library, *L'Italo Americano* newspaper, Los Angeles City Archives, Carolyn Cole of the Los Angeles Public Library, the *Los Angeles Times*, Monterey Park Historical Society, Plaza Methodist Church, Linda Desiante of the Sons of Italy Hollywood, Donna Angiuli, Fr. Giovanni Bizotto and Fr. Raniero Alessandrini at St. Peter's Italian Church, University of California Irvine Library, and the University of Michigan.

INTRODUCTION

This text presents a history of Los Angeles's Little Italy during the 100-year period following the arrival of the city's first Italian pioneer in 1827, a topic that has been examined by fewer than a handful of historians over the past 50 years. Italian Americans, like other groups, left a lasting impression on the city's social, economic, and cultural fabric and contributed to Los Angeles's development as one of the world's greatest metropolises.

The Italian presence in the American West can be traced to the 14th century with Fr. Marco da Nizza, who participated in Francisco Vásquez Coronado's expedition in search of the mythical Seven Cities of Gold. In 1542, Bartolomeo Ferrelo, of Portuguese-Italian ancestry, explored the California coast as a navigator for Juan Rodriguez Cabrillo. In the years that followed, Italian friars Saverio Saetta, Giovanni Salvaterra (whose name is commonly written Juan Maria Salvatierra), and Eusebio Chino played instrumental roles in the colonization of California through the mission system. As a result of his extensive travels and thorough research, Chino, a Sicilian frequently described as the "Padre on Horseback," proved that Baja California was a peninsula, not an elongated island as was popularly believed. Explorations by Fr. Giovanni ("Juan") Crespi led to the European world's discovery of the San Francisco Bay in 1772. Father Crespi, who said the first Catholic mass in Southern California, was the official diarist of the Portola expedition, which explored Alta California and established the famed El Camino Real trail. On August 2, 1769, Crespi wrote in his journal of a "beautiful river from the northwest" that he called El Rio de Nuestra Señora la Reina de Los Angeles de Porciúncula, or "the River of Our Lady the Queen of the Angels of the Porciuncúla." *Porciúncula* is a corruption of the archaic Italian *porziuncola*, meaning "small parcel." Today this river is known simply as "the L.A. River."

During the period of Spanish rule in California, which lasted until 1821, the number of Italians in the region was small compared to other nationalities. Italian families of the colonial era were so deeply integrated in California's Hispanic culture that their identities as *Californios* often superseded that as Italians. The Bandini family, settlers of what would become San Diego and whose surname is synonymous with the state's early history, best exemplify this phenomenon. It was not until California became part of the newly independent Mexico, however, that Italian immigration to the region increased and permanent Italian settlement in Los Angeles took root.

While conducting historical research is often compared to detective work, chronicling Los Angeles's early Italian community is more accurately likened to chasing ghosts. Although Los Angeles possesses the nation's fifth-largest Italian community today, little physical evidence of the original Italian enclaves remains. Historic Little Italy is masked by Chinatown and Olvera Street. As a consequence of redevelopment and the construction of the Hollywood and Golden State Freeways, the homes, buildings, and streets that witnessed the city's Italian history were destroyed. In some cases, the entire enclave was erased from the map. Little Italy could be said to have received a double interment; the first was physical, the second psychological. The Los Angeles Italian community, humble and progress-minded, educated and prosperous, seldom took the time to preserve their history or ensure that it received adequate representation. When they severed their ties to the old neighborhood, many Italians simply never looked back.

Some assert that Italians have reached the twilight of their ethnicity, a stage during which their cultural distinctiveness remains visible, but only faintly so. Simultaneously, however, third- and fourth-generation Italians are rediscovering, or perhaps exploring, their ethnic heritage for the first time. Should history prove as inextricably connected to memory as it is to place, the creation of the Italian American Museum in the historic Italian Hall on North Main Street, the oldest existing structure from the city's historic Little Italy, promises to assist Italians in this journey and provide all visitors with a more meaningful understanding of the multi-layered history of Los Angeles and that of the nation.

One

THE PIONEERS

When people speak of Italian immigration to the United States, rarely is Los Angeles the city that comes to mind. Usually they envision huddled peasants in New York's teeming slums whose lives have become familiar through Hollywood films or whose immigration stories are typically situated on the Eastern seaboard. The Los Angeles Italian immigration experience proves remarkable in the numerous respects in which it differs from that of their compatriots in other parts of the country. Given the degree to which Italian Americans have achieved social acceptance and upward mobility, it may be difficult to conceive that during the 19th and early 20th centuries, Italians, confined to the nation's immigrant underclass, faced considerable prejudice and hostility. Referred to pejoratively as "dagos" and "wops," during the 1800s, Italians were the second most common targets of lynching in the United States.

This was not the case in Los Angeles, however. Established as a colonial outpost of Spain, until the last quarter of the 19th century, Los Angeles remained a city profoundly influenced by its Spanish and Mexican roots. Sharing a common "Latin" culture, Mexican Los Angeles embraced its Italian pioneers. In the early 19th century, the cost of the transatlantic journey to Los Angeles equaled or surpassed an immigrant's yearly earnings. The price and arduousness of the voyage, combined with Los Angeles's isolation (especially prior to 1869, when the transcontinental railroad linked Los Angeles to the rest to the country), made the city a destination for few, and the Italian population remained small compared to New York or Boston. While Italian immigrants elsewhere in the nation were frequently sojourners—immigrants who intended to return to their homeland after making their "little piece" in America—Los Angeles's Italians came with the intention of remaining.

Los Angeles's first Little Italy was located in the historic center of the city in what is today El Pueblo de Los Angeles Historical Monument. There, in 1781, settlers from present-day Mexico, recruited by the Spanish crown, established an agricultural community to sustain Spain's influence. In the area surrounding the town's plaza, the settlers, including some of Los Angeles's wealthiest residents, built adobe homes. By the mid-1800s, the town had become increasingly multiethnic. Italians lived side by side with the Mexican, French, and Chinese communities.

The first Italian settler in Los Angeles was 31-year-old sailor Giovanni Leandri, a native of Sardinia who arrived in 1827, fifty-four years after Los Angeles's founding. Leandri built an adobe home and established a general store on Calle de los Negros. Pictured above in 1882, Calle de los Negros later became part of North Los Angeles Street. (Courtesy of the Los Angeles Public Library.)

During the 19th century, Spanish remained the lingua franca of Los Angeles. Italian settlers often learned Spanish before they learned English. Presumably, similarities between the two tongues facilitated language acquisition and eased the acculturation process. Many of the city's Italian pioneers, including Leandri, also assumed Spanish names. Within a decade of his arrival, Leandri was known as Juan Leandry as this 1836 deed for his property on Calle de Los Negros illustrates. (Courtesy of the Los Angeles City Archive.)

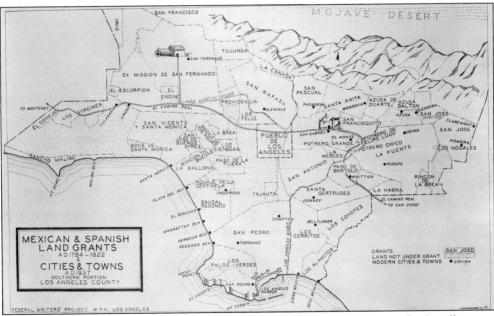

The high incidence of marriage between Italians and the Latino community further illustrates the hospitable social climate Italians encountered in the pueblo. In 1839, Leandri married the daughter of a Californio family, Maria Francesca Uribe, and was named the Los Angeles pueblo's *juez de paz* (justice of the peace) the following year. Leandri then purchased Rancho Los Coyotes, identified on the bottom right of the map, an almost 50,000-acre property in present-day Buena Park (northern Orange County) where he built another adobe home. (Courtesy of the Los Angeles Public Library, WPA Collection.)

Leandri renamed the rancho La Buena Esperanza, Spanish for "the good hope." More than 6,000 head of cattle grazed on Leandri's ranch (above) and the meat, hide, and tallow that they produced made Leandri one of the pueblo's most prominent residents. At the time of his death in 1843, Leandri's estate was valued at over $30,000. (Courtesy of the Buena Park Historical Society.)

In 1834, Matteo Sabichi, a native of Genoa, settled in Los Angles after living first in Monterey. He too built a home on the southeast side of the Plaza, which would later be known as the Del Valle adobe, and married the daughter of a prominent Californio family, Josefa Coronel (left). Josefa's brother, Antonio Coronel, was a respected city official who served as *alcalde* (mayor) and later as California state treasurer. (Courtesy of the University of California, Irvine.)

The couple had two children: Matteo, born in 1841, and Francesco (right), born in 1842. Francesco married Magdalena Wolfskill, the daughter of pioneer William Wolfskill, and together they had eight children. (Courtesy of the University of California, Irvine.)

Fluent in three languages, Francesco served on the Los Angeles City Council in the 1870s and 1880s. (Courtesy of the Los Angeles City Archive.)

Francesco Sabichi's house, located in the fashionable West Adams District, is a testimony to the success and wealth that the family enjoyed. (Courtesy of the Los Angeles Public Library.)

The city of Montebello, located 8 miles east of downtown Los Angeles, was once the ranch of the reclusive Italian pioneer Alessandro Repetto, a Genoese who had been a doctor in the Italian army. In 1866, Repetto acquired 5,000 acres of land from Don Antonio Lugo, where he raised sheep and cattle. Fugitive Tiburcio Vasquez, believed by many to be the inspiration for Johnston McCulley's character Zorro, appeared at Repetto's ranch (above) in 1874 and demanded $800 to finance a revolution in Baja California. With only $80 in coin, Repetto issued a check, which he sent to town with his young nephew. (Courtesy of the Monterey Park Historical Society.)

Vasquez, pictured, warned the lad that if he returned with the authorities, Repetto would be killed. The president of the Temple Bank in Los Angeles grew suspicious. After questioning the child, what was transpiring at the ranch became apparent and law enforcement was alerted. The sheriff's posse was detected as they approached the hills of San Gabriel, and Vasquez, the infamous bandit/freedom fighter, fled, leaving Repetto unscathed.

While anti-Catholic sentiment prevailed on the East Coast, in El Pueblo de la Reina de Los Angeles (the Town of the Queen of the Angels), where Catholicism was the de facto religion, Italians practiced their faith without fear of reprisal and were represented among the city's religious leaders. In 1857, Neapolitan Fr. Blas Raho was appointed pastor of Our Lady Queen of Angels Church, the oldest Catholic church in Los Angeles, pictured on the left, completed in 1822. Father Raho was a respected member of the community who worked tirelessly to restore the church in the 1860s. (Courtesy of the Los Angeles Public Library.)

Other than the usual ports of entry, such as Ellis Island and Louisiana, Italian pioneers often arrived in the pueblo via South America and Mexico. Early Italian settlers tended to be northern Italian and were skilled workers or artisans. In 1853, Genoese brothers Giovanni and Mateo LanFranco settled in the Los Angeles Pueblo after stopping briefly in Lima, Peru, and New York. Within a year, the brothers had established a grocery store on Main Street near Commercial Street (above), just north of where Los Angeles City Hall stands. (Courtesy of the Los Angeles Public Library.)

Like his contemporaries, Giovanni (left) married a Mexican American woman, Petra Pilar Sepulveda, whose family owned Rancho Palos Verdes, a community located in southwest Los Angeles. Prior to the arrival of Italian women to Los Angeles in the last quarter of the 19th century, most Italian men found their brides almost exclusively in the Mexican community, intermarrying with Mexicans more than any other European group.

In 1866, the brothers, who had achieved great success as merchants and forwarding agents, built the stately LanFranco Building in the heart of Los Angeles's commercial center. While the LanFranco Building no longer stands, the family's legacy can be detected in East Los Angeles, where a street bearing the LanFranco name runs between Fourth Street and Whittier Boulevard. (Courtesy of the Los Angeles Public Library.)

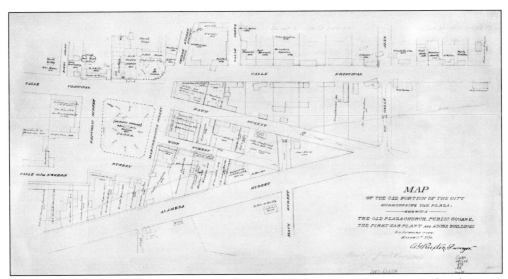

Southern California's Mediterranean climate led many immigrants to engage in agricultural pursuits in Los Angeles. Their endeavors played an integral role in the region's economic development. By 1869, Los Angeles was the wine capital of California, producing four million gallons of wine annually. The thriving wineries of prominent Italian winemakers including Giuseppe Gazza and Giovanni Covacicci were responsible for Olvera Street to originally be named Calle de las Vignas, or Wine Street, as depicted on this 1873 map.

The majority of the city's Italian pioneers were transmigrants who worked and lived elsewhere before settling in Los Angeles. This served to create an Italian community that, in addition to being hearty and resolute, was better acclimated to the ways of *L'America*. Antonio Pelanconi, a native of Piedmont, traversed the continent and arrived in Los Angeles in 1853. He associated himself with vintner Giovanni Gazza, who owned a winery on Calle de las Vignas. Pelanconi soon became the sole proprietor of the winery, which would later be known as the Pelanconi House. (Courtesy of the Historic Italian Hall Foundation.)

Built by Giuseppe Covacicci (also spelled Covacci, Cavacichi, and Covasich) between 1855 and 1857, the Pelanconi House is the oldest extant brick building in Los Angeles and home to a popular Mexican restaurant. In 1877, Calle de las Vignas was renamed Olvera Street in honor of Agustín Olvera, the first judge of the city and county of Los Angeles. (Author's collection.)

On March 4, 1866, Pelanconi married a Californio woman, Isabel Ramirez (right), and together they had eight children: Lorenzo, Magdalena, Honorina, Antonio, Maria, Lucia, Petra, and Antonio (second of the same name). In the early years of their marriage, the family lived on the second story of the Pelanconi House. The first floor of the house featured a large, exposed basement for the storage of wine and brandy. Isabel Pelanconi was one of the best-educated women of Los Angeles in her day as well as an astute businesswoman. (Courtesy of El Pueblo Historical Monument.)

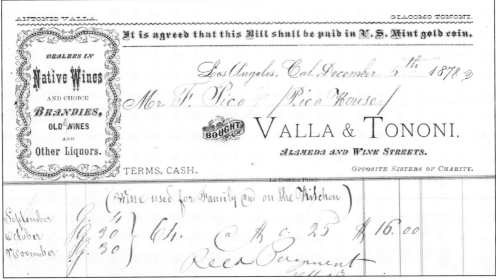

Pelanconi remained the owner of the winery until 1877, when he sold the business to Antonio Valla and Giacomo Tononi in order to dedicate more time to his ranch in Tropico, which is today Glendale, a city northeast of Los Angeles. A public park and street in Glendale memorialize the Pelanconi name. Two years after her husband's death in 1879, Isabel married his former business partner, Giacomo Tononi. (Courtesy of the Historic Italian Hall Foundation.)

Handsome Lorenzo Pelanconi, the eldest son of Isabel and Antonio Pelanconi, was born Christmas Day, 1866. (Courtesy of the Historic Italian Hall Foundation.)

Despite his status as the son of one of Los Angeles's most prominent families, Lorenzo worked as a clerk in the winery before marrying the daughter of a Southern California Spanish family, Martina Yorba, after whom the Orange County city of Yorba Linda is named. In 1914, he built a central portion of what is referred to as the Old Winery at 845 North Alameda Street. Today an art gallery belonging to the City of Los Angeles and El Paseo, a popular restaurant, occupy the site. (Courtesy of the Anaheim Public Library.)

Brothers Giovanni and Carlo Demateis Winery leased the Valla-Tononi Winery in 1899 and renamed it the North Cucamonga Winery. (Courtesy of the Demateis family.)

Pictured from left to right, Carlo Demateis, Filippo Fava, an unidentified worker, and Giovanni Demateis pose in front of the winery in the early 1900s. (Courtesy of the Demateis family.)

Gold fever drew significant numbers of Italians to California. Some of them settled in Los Angeles after testing their fate in gold country. Ambrosio Vignolo, pictured with family members, was one such Italian. Born to a poor family in Italy in 1828, Vignolo spent six months in Boston before setting sail around Cape Horn and settling in California in 1872, where he pursued mining as an occupation and achieved considerable wealth. (Courtesy of the Historic Italian Hall Foundation.)

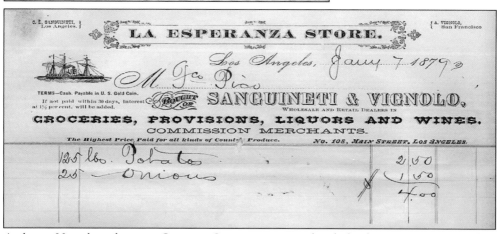

Ambrosio Vignolo and partner Giovanni Sanguinetti opened a wholesale grocery store named La Esperanza, Spanish for "the hope." Located on North Main Street, just north of present-day Los Angeles City Hall, La Esperanza supplied groceries to many local businesses. Vignolo's success in the grocery business allowed him to purchase considerable amounts of land. He served as city assessor from 1882 to 1884 and later became a director of the International Savings Bank. Notice that the total amount paid for 125 pounds of potatoes and 25 pounds of onions was $4. (Courtesy of the Historic Italian Hall Foundation.)

The Pico House, located at 424 North Main Street, was one client of Vignolo and Sanguinetti's La Esperanza store. Built between 1869 and 1870, the Pico House was Los Angeles's first three-story building and first elegant hotel. (Author's collection.)

Perhaps the most infamous of the Italian pioneers, Bartolo Ballerino came to Los Angeles via Chile in the late 1850s, when Los Angeles averaged one murder per day and was considered the wildest town west of the Rockies. He opened a restaurant and saloon at 422 Calle de Los Negros, which, by the 1860s, comprised the core of the city's vice district, complete with opium dens and raucous gambling houses. After partnering with former San Francisco Democratic Party boss Chris Buckley, Ballerino built an empire on the sex trade, which earned him the nickname "the Crib King." In 1896, Ballerino's land holdings were estimated to value $250,000 and included acreage in Pico Heights, a ranch in the Hollywood Hills, and his crib properties, from which he collected magnificent rents. (Courtesy of Dr. Walter Lindley Scrapbooks, Special Collections, Honnold/Mudd Library at Claremont College.)

Prostitution was tolerated in Los Angeles as long as it remained confined to the red light district, which, by the late 1880s, was located southeast of the Plaza, along North Alameda and Aliso Streets. While madam-run brothels had previously been the norm, by the 1890s, the majority of the sex trade took place in cribs, complexes of small, sparsely furnished, single rooms, such as those pictured here. (Courtesy of the Los Angeles Public Library, Security Pacific Bank Collection.)

Serving a diverse clientele that ranged from elected officials to wandering husbands, an estimated 300 cribs existed in the city at the time, among which Ballerino's International Hotel, pictured here, was the largest. When progressive reformers besieged the crib industry in 1903, prompting crackdowns from law enforcement, Ballerino and other crib owners found loopholes. Advertising "lace work" and "massage" and transforming cribs into "cigar stores" and "neckwear shops," Ballerino postponed his inevitable demise until the following year, when he was prosecuted for renting property for immoral purposes. Though the cribs along Alameda closed, the prostitution industry found a new locale nearby. (Courtesy of the Los Angeles Public Library, Security Pacific Bank Collection.)

Two

SETTLEMENT AND ACCULTURATION

The last four decades of the 19th century was a period of significant change for Los Angeles. Following the United States' war with Mexico, the Gold Rush, and a severe drought that killed cattle herds, the city's Mexican and Californio community lost considerable wealth and power. The completion of the Southern Pacific Railroad in 1876, which connected San Francisco and Los Angeles, brought settlers from the East, and the city's population grew substantially, from approximately 4,400 in 1860 to 50,000 in 1890. As the business district and civic center moved south, the Plaza area rapidly deteriorated into a slum, where most residents were either recent immigrants or the impoverished. Despite its reputation and perhaps out of economic necessity, Italians continued to settle in Ward Eight—the Plaza area and its surrounding streets—including Lyon, Date, San Fernando (now North Spring), and North Main Streets, where the melodic sound of Italian could be heard alongside Spanish, French, Chinese, and English.

Bruno and Sotello Streets, which bear the names of early Italian settlers and intersect North Spring Street near Los Angeles State Historic Park, still exist today. Other streets named after pioneer Italian resident Nicola Quierolo and Giuseppe Garibaldi, the leader of Italian unification, were erased from the map when the Twin Towers Correctional Facility and the Men's Central Jail were built. During these years, a growing number of Italians also settled in Ward Two, the northernmost area of the city, which adjoined the Eighth Ward. The foothills of Elysian Park, including present-day Chinatown (then known as Sonoratown), Chavez Ravine (current site of Dodger Stadium), Solano Canyon, and Victor Heights comprise the core of the old Second Ward.

By 1890, Italian-owned businesses such as Tognetti's Cigar Factory; Giacomo Castruccio's Mariposa Store; Martinoli's Bakery; Madame Zuccha's Restaurant, Hotel Roma; Giambastini and Fazzi's Wood, Coal, Hay, and Grain store; and Carbello and Garcia's Construction Company dotted the city's landscape. At the turn of the 20th century, *La Colonia*, as the Italian community was known, with a population that neared 2,000, possessed a mutual benefit organization and an Italian-language newspaper and had forged ties that transcended *campanilismo*, the mother country's insidious provincialism. Albeit less nucleated and homogeneous, Los Angeles's Italian enclaves, like the Little Italy neighborhoods elsewhere in the nation, functioned as an extension of the homeland and eased the immigrant's transition between peasants and "urban villagers."

While most Italians in Ward Eight were renters, home ownership in Ward Two, where Italians could purchase homes for as little as $100, was higher. This 1886 photograph of the intersection of Bellevue Avenue (now Sunset Boulevard) and Buena Vista Street (now Broadway) depicts the types of homes that would have been owned by Italians during the era. (Courtesy of the Los Angeles Public Library, Herald Examiner Collection.)

Early residents of Bellevue Street included the Costantini family, who immigrated to Los Angeles from Asti, Piedmont, in 1892. From left to right are Gioachino, Lorenzo (seated) with baby Maria Lucia in his lap, Vincenzo, and Angela Maria Costantini. Baby Maria died six weeks after her birth. The family, who Americanized their name to Constantine, later moved to 712 New High Street in the Second Ward and 18 Olvera Street in the Eighth Ward. (Courtesy of Marsha Johnson.)

The long-demolished Sunset Hotel once stood on San Fernando and Ord Streets. Then predominantly Italian and Mexican, Ord Street is the heart of Chinatown today. (Courtesy of the Los Angeles Public Library, Security Pacific Bank Collection.)

The Peluffo grocery and general merchandise store, located at 705 New High Street in the Second Ward, was founded in 1894. The family was among the first in the city to own an automobile. (Courtesy of the Los Angeles Public Library, Security Pacific Bank Collection.)

In 1898, brothers Giovanni and Lorenzo Fazzi established the Fort Market at 614–616 Macy Street (present-day Cesar Chavez Avenue). Named after Fort Moore, the Mexican-American War site where U.S. forces built a stronghold during the invasion of Los Angeles, the Fort Market was a grocery store and butcher shop. (Courtesy of Roy and Helene Fazzi.)

In the late 1800s, the ethnically diverse residents of Chavez Ravine included Italians who herded goats and sheep within the city limits. (Courtesy of John Nese/Galco's Old World Grocery.)

Roughly 10 percent of the city's Italian population, most of whom were fishermen from the islands of Ischia and Sicily, lived in San Pedro, where they established the foundation for the thriving local fishing and canning industry. (Courtesy of S. Ben Piazza.)

Frequently immigrants resided with family members who had already settled in the area or lived in boardinghouses with *paesani* who hailed from neighboring, if not the same, villages in Italy. Giuseppe Maga (first row, center) and Giacomo Castellano (first row, right) along with other immigrants from Scarmagno, Piedmont, pose in front of the boardinghouse where they lived in the Eighth Ward. (Courtesy of Elda Maga Pilj.)

Boardinghouses played a significant role in the acculturation process, where newly arrived immigrants procured employment, obtained the information necessary to navigate their new surroundings, and continued to practice a common, albeit transplanted, culture. Upon their arrival to Los Angeles, the Arconti family, who came from Lonate Pozzolo, Lombardy, lived in this boardinghouse on Bauchet Street, the current site of the Terminal Annex Post Office. Pictured from left to right are Jean, Mary, and Lee Arconti. (Courtesy of the Arconti family.)

The Aprato family, seen here seated in front of a boardinghouse located on Ord Street, was one of many families from the town of Bosconero, Piedmont, that immigrated to Los Angeles. (Courtesy of David and Juliette Aprato.)

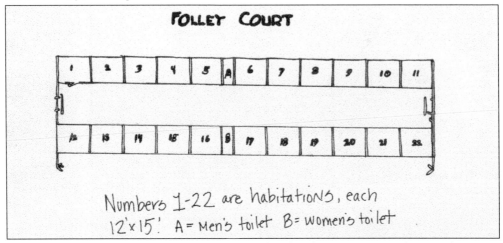

The most destitute members of the community lived in housing courts, clusters of 10 to 20 shack-like bungalows that were situated on a single lot and faced a common yard. The average dwelling was approximately 250 square feet, typically had two rooms, and was shared by four or more people. Communal toilets and water taps were located in the courtyard, as the residences usually lacked indoor plumbing and seldom had gas or oil stoves for heat and food preparation. On average, residents paid $7 a month in rent for such accommodations while earning a daily wage of $2. The Folley Court, located at 742 New High Street, was considered among the worst of its time. (Author's collection.)

The squalor of the housing courts made them the frequent targets of reformers, including Jacob Riis, who likened them to the tenement slums of the East. A member of the Los Angeles Italian community recalls living in the dirt-paved McKinney Court, once located on the 2100 block of East Seventh Street, as a child. In absence of indoor plumbing, he bathed using one of the court's few water taps. (Courtesy of the Los Angeles Public Library, Security Pacific Bank Collection.)

The McKinney Court's 70 residents shared eight toilets. While many faced the stark reality of poverty, Italians comprised only 4 percent of families receiving county aid. (Courtesy of the Los Angeles Public Library, Security Pacific Bank Collection.)

This 1890s view of Main Street looking south from Olvera Street captures the diversity of the Eighth Ward. At the center of the photograph, a Chinese father and his two children, both in traditional dress, stroll amid the bustle of the Mexican Plaza. To the left is the Pico House, which was then owned and operated by Giuseppe Pagliano. Belgian F. W. Braun's Drug Company, one of the earliest pharmaceutical companies in Los Angeles, is on the right. (Courtesy of El Pueblo de Los Angeles Historical Monument.)

One building south, Dalmatian Giovanni "John" Lopizich, in partnership with a Frenchman, owned the Viole-Lopizich Pharmacy. (Courtesy of the Historic Italian Hall Foundation.)

Though best known for its Mexican history, in the late 1800s and early 1900s, Italians owned or operated one-third of the buildings that today comprise El Pueblo Historical Monument. It was there that Secondo Guasti, whose name is synonymous with numerous Southern California place names, including the Inland Empire city and the Guasti Villa on Adams Boulevard in Los Angeles, secured one of his first jobs after arriving in 1883. (Courtesy of the Historic Italian Hall Foundation.)

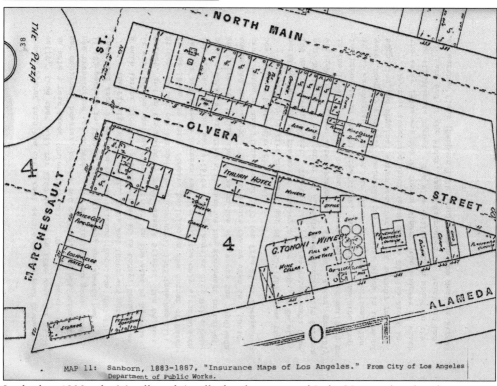

MAP 11: Sanborn, 1883-1887, "Insurance Maps of Los Angeles." From City of Los Angeles Department of Public Works.

In the late 1800s, the Morelli and Amillo families operated Italia Unita, a hotel and restaurant located in the Avila Adobe on Olvera Street, the oldest extant residence in the city. Guasti, a cook at the restaurant, would later marry Luisa Amillo, the proprietor's daughter.

After establishing two successful vineyards in the pueblo, Guasti, along with 15 of his countrymen, purchased extensive acreage in the then-remote Rancho Cucamonga, a community located 40 miles east of Los Angeles. At 5,000 acres, Guasti's vineyard, the Italian Vineyard Company, was the largest in the world. From penniless immigrant to "Wine King," Guasti best exemplifies the entrepreneurial spirit of the era. The native of Mombaruzzo, Piedmont, would become one of the world's wealthiest men. Guasti was active in numerous Italian organizations and, arguably, was the community's most generous benefactor. (Courtesy of the Los Angeles Public Library, Works Progress Administration Collection.)

Working "at Guasti" was a rite of passage for thousands of Italian and, later, Mexican immigrants. In addition to providing homes for his workers, Guasti built a school, market, bakery, library, fire station, doctor's office, and a host of shops. (Courtesy of Elda Maga Pilj.)

Guasti's workforce included a significant number of women. (Courtesy of the Los Angeles Public Library, Works Progress Administration Collection.)

In 1909, Guasti held a fund-raiser for a night school in Los Angeles that taught English to Italian immigrants. He chartered a train to transport the 1,200 guests to his town for the event. (Courtesy of the Historic Italian Hall Foundation.)

Shareholders of the Italian Vineyard Company photographed during an early-1900s retreat included the families of Giovanni Gai, Joseph Pagliano, and Angelo Bessolo. (Courtesy of the Historic Italian Hall Foundation.)

Secondo Guasti's Beaux Arts–style residence located at 2700 West Adams Street is a Los Angeles Historic-Cultural Monument. (Courtesy of the Los Angeles Public Library, Security Pacific Bank Collection.)

Guasti spared no expense when constructing his Los Angeles home, designed in 1910 and built over a period of four years, which was the site of countless parties for movie stars and dignitaries, including Benito Mussolini's son. (Courtesy of the Los Angeles Public Library, Security Pacific Bank Collection.)

What Guasti was to grapes, Sicilian immigrant Domenico Jebbia was to bananas. Jebbia, known as the "Banana King," established the West Coast Banana Distributing Company at the Los Angeles Produce Market in 1886. A simple, unpretentious man, Jebbia's request to join the exclusive Los Angeles Midwick Country Club (which had a membership list that included Walt Disney and Spencer Tracy) was denied. When the property was later offered for sale by auction, Jebbia, clad in overalls, purchased the 200-acre club with $178,000 cash—bundled together in wads and stuffed into his pockets.

Joseph F. Sartori was among the most powerful figures in Los Angeles during the first half of the 20th century. After completing a Juris Doctorate degree at the University of Michigan in 1881, he moved to Los Angeles, where he founded the First National Bank in 1887 and, two years later, the Security Trust and Savings Bank. Security Trust and Savings Bank was the financial institution responsible for the expansion of the downtown business district and early development projects, such as the construction of the Biltmore Hotel and the Subway Terminal Building, as well as the extension of the Pacific Electric Railway line to the San Fernando Valley. Diminutive in stature, Sartori often had his furnishings (including his bathtub) custom made. Sartori died in 1946; in 1993, Bank of America absorbed Security Pacific National Bank. (Courtesy of the Los Angeles Public Library, Herald Examiner Collection.)

At the dawn of the 20th century, the *Los Angeles Times* frequently highlighted the activities of the vibrant Italian community, including an elaborate parade and celebration for the 400th anniversary of Columbus's voyages to the Americas. (Courtesy of the Los Angeles Public Library, Security Pacific Bank Collection.)

Diverse audiences of Angelenos enjoyed Italian opera, which was first introduced to the city during the last quarter of the 19th century. (Courtesy of the Historic Italian Hall Foundation.)

In 1877, Ambrosio Vignolo and Antonio Pelanconi founded La Società Italiana di Mutua Beneficenza (the Italian Mutual Benefit Society), a group that assisted immigrants in finding housing and employment and provided for its members in times of need. Within three years, the group boasted 80 members and as early as 1883 had its own meeting hall in the heart of Little Italy at 730 and 732 Buena Vista Street, now North Broadway. (Courtesy of the *Los Angeles Times*.)

In 1888, a second group comprised of younger men was founded under Vignolo's direction, La Societá Unione e Fratellanza Garibaldina (the Garibaldina Society of Unity and Brotherhood), named after the Italian patriot Giuseppe Garibaldi. The Garibaldina Society originally gathered at the Sepulveda House on Olvera Street. Its philanthropic efforts ranged from providing assistance to the infirm and indigent to supporting the Italian Red Cross and aiding World War I veterans. Part of the Italian American Museum of Los Angeles's collection, this Garibaldina Mutual Benefit Society ribbon was worn during banquets, parades, and other events. (Courtesy of the Arconti family.)

The philanthropic society, which celebrated their 200th anniversary in 2008, is the oldest Italian organization in the city. Headquartered today in Highland Park, a neighborhood in northeast Los Angeles, the society organizes fund-raisers, bocce tournaments, excursions, and themed dinners. (Courtesy of the Garibaldina Mutual Benefit Society.)

OUR ITALIA'S PRESS BORN.

Music and Wine Over "La Colonia Italiana."

Editor Carlo Abrato Hands Out First Copics.

Only Paper of Its Tongue in the Southland.

To the cheers and bravos of assembled banqueters of the enthusiastic Latin race handed over wine glasses to the eager recipients by its editor, Carlo Abrato, a new Los Angeles

JNO. B. ZUCHELLI,
Toastmaster.

newspaper. "La Colonia Italiana," made its initial public appearance last night.

The new publication. issued in the interests of the Italian colony of Southern California and contiguous

As early as 1894, Los Angeles possessed an Italian-language newspaper, *L'Eco della Colonia*, founded by Gabrielle Spini. Another Italian-language newspaper, *La Colonia Italiana*, exited the press soon thereafter. Issued weekly by the Italian Publishing Company, the paper was headquartered in Little Italy at 611 North San Fernando Street. (Courtesy of the *Los Angeles Times*.)

42

Three

ITALIAN LOS ANGELES
1900–1927

Mamma, dammi cento lire. Voglio andare a L'America
Figlio mio, L' America . . . No! No! No!
Cento lire te gli darei, a L'America non andare!

Mother, give me a hundred lire because I want to go to America.
My son, not America!
I will give you a hundred lire, but don't go to America!

First appearing in the late 1800s, the folk song above was familiar to Italian immigrants across the diaspora and expressed the agony that families felt surrounding the exodus of loved ones. Taking nothing but the possessions they could carry, between 1876 and 1914, fourteen million people left Italy—one-third of the country's population. Few other countries have experienced a greater hemorrhaging of their populace in such a short period. What provoked masses of Italians to leave all they had known for a land they had scarcely seen in photographs?

The answer to this question can be found in the desperate nature of the Italian peasant's existence, economic and political inequities following Italy's unification, and the series of calamities that struck the country between 1875 and 1920. Located at the crossroads of civilizations, for centuries, the Italian peninsula was divided into feuding states ruled by foreign powers. Hereditary land possession determined an individual's political power and social status, providing the majority of Italians with little hope of improving their lives. Italians referred to their condition as *la miseria*, or "the misery," which was not a temporary state of mind but a pervasive feature of daily life. Italian peasants lived in abject poverty, earning on average only 31¢ for working a 12-hour day, a wage that proves even bleaker when one considers that sugar cost 19¢ a pound.

A colloquial greeting during this era was *hai mangiato*, which translated literally means "have you eaten?" Pellagra and cholera claimed many peasant lives. Between 1890 and 1894, twenty percent of the population of Basilicata, one of the poorest regions in Southern Italy, succumbed to malaria. A series of earthquakes and subsequent tidal waves struck the *Mezzogiorno* in the late 1800s and early 1900s, leveling entire villages and killing hundreds of thousands. Meanwhile, plagues of insects decimated crops and pushed peasants to the brink of starvation. Sharing a fate similar to immigrants today, Italian peasants had two choices: stay and starve or leave. Four of the 14 million who left selected the United States to be their home.

By 1910, Italians constituted one-third of the residents of Elysian Park and present-day Chinatown, where they were most concentrated on the 500–800 blocks of Castelar Street (now North Hill Street), as well as on Alpine Street, Casanova Street, and North Broadway. Frank Capra lived on Castelar Street, shown here in 1920, during his childhood. At age six, the *It's a Wonderful Life* director sold newspapers on North Main Street and attended Castelar Street Elementary, which was then characterized by the *Los Angeles Times* as an "Italian school." (Courtesy of the Los Angeles Public Library, Security Pacific Bank Collection.)

Dogtown, an enclave located between the Plaza and Lincoln Heights, derived its name from an early Los Angeles animal shelter located in close proximity. Many of the neighborhood's Italian and Mexican residents, such as those pictured here, worked for Southern Pacific and Santa Fe Railroads. While the settlement patterns of early Italian immigrants influenced the areas in which 20th-century Italians established their homes, restrictive racial covenants also played a role. Designed to enforce segregation, racial covenants barred racial, ethnic, and religious minorities from owning property in parts of the city. (Courtesy of El Pueblo de Los Angeles Historical Monument/William Mason Collection.)

Most commonly applied to African Americans, the covenants also excluded other groups including Latinos, Asians, Jews, Muslims, and Italians from home ownership in areas such as the San Fernando Valley and West Los Angeles until 1948, when the Supreme Court invalidated racial covenants in *Shelley v. Kramer* and *Hurd v. Hodge*. Former residents of Alpine Street, including the Pontrelli and Manciapinto (Mance) families, pictured on the right, recall the feelings of comfort and connectivity that Little Italy provided as opposed to a sense of marginalization. (Courtesy of Dr. William Fasoli.)

Coinciding with the completion of the Panama Canal, the Italian population of Los Angeles rose steadily, from approximately 2,000 in 1900 to 3,800 in 1910 and 12,700 in 1930. In the Second Ward, neighbors could be heard calling to one another in Italian, reporting on the whereabouts of each other's children, and exchanging recipes in a neighborhood that was almost exclusively Italian. Pictured are the Pontrelli, Mance, and Rabaglino families with an unidentified priest. (Courtesy of Dr. William Fasoli.)

In the early 1900s, Little Italy continued to expand eastward into Lincoln Heights. Darwin, Mozart, and Sichel Streets, as well as Avenues Eighteen and Nineteen, comprised the core of the enclave, which at its peak possessed 8,000 Italian residents and was the largest Italian neighborhood in the city. The Gatto and Cortese families, from Cosenza, Calabria, and Lucca Sicula, Sicily, settled in Lincoln Heights after first having lived in Louisiana, Pennsylvania, and Pueblo, Colorado. Recognizing Pueblo offered her sons no future, Mary Gatto (pictured above at her wedding) urged her husband to relocate the family to Los Angeles. Large numbers of Pueblo's residents settled Lincoln Heights in the 1940s. (Author's collection.)

Residents of Bauchet Street, including the Festa, Emanuelli, and Lombardo families, celebrate Armistice Day. The word *pace* (pronounced pah-chay) is Italian for "peace." Today the Men's Central Jail occupies the site. (Courtesy of Bruce Festa.)

The Pagone family, who originally hailed from Bari, Puglia, settled in Dogtown at 114 Sotello Street. (Courtesy of Mike Pagone.)

In the Sixth and Seventh Wards, just south of downtown near Alameda and Ninth Streets, an enclave of mostly Sicilian immigrants hailing from the towns of Piana dei Greci (now Piana degli Albanesi), Contessa Entellina, Santa Cristina Gela, and Corleone lived in close vicinity to the Los Angeles City Market. There they were most concentrated on Hunter, Enterprise, Lemon, and Wilson Streets. In addition to Italian, many of the enclave's residents spoke *Ghè Ghè*, a dialect of Arberesh, the language spoken by groups of Albanians who had founded settlements in Sicily in the late 1400s. A number of Italians also lived in Boyle Heights, which, in the 1910s, was home to the city's Jewish, Japanese, and Russian communities. (Courtesy of the Los Angeles Public Library.)

Ricci, Del Beato, and Borgia were three of Little Italy's most popular photography studios. In the early 1900s, this group of Italian businessmen sought the services of Nick Borgia, whose studio was located on San Fernando Street. After taking their wedding photographs at Ricci Studio, Italian couples purchased their wedding cakes at Giacchino's Bakery, which was located on the same block of North Broadway and was famous for their rum cakes. (Courtesy of James Frieda.)

Though separated geographically from Los Angeles proper, the San Pedro Italian community flourished, fueled by the booming fishing industry. In the early 1900s, the Costantini family left the Eighth Ward and settled among paesani in San Pedro, where they opened a grocery store on Third and Palos Verdes Streets. (Courtesy of Marsha Johnson.)

Rancho San Pedro was the site of the first Spanish land grant awarded to Juan Jose Dominguez in 1794. In the late 1800s, drawn to the fishing industry, Portuguese, Italian, Greek, and Croatian families established a vibrant community in the hills surrounding the harbor. Established in 1889, San Pedro's Mary Star of the Sea Church is one of the oldest churches in the Los Angeles Archdiocese. It is known as the "fisherman's parish" because of its relationship to the port and San Pedro's fishing community. (Courtesy of the Los Angeles Public Library.)

In 1937, San Pedro's fishing fleet numbered 500 boats, and the community was home to 16 canneries. (Courtesy of S. Ben Piazza.)

While Little Italy expanded, the community's ties to the Plaza, the area in which the earliest Italians settled, remained intact. Subsequent to Pio Pico losing his hotel to foreclosure, Giuseppe Pagliano (center) purchased the property and maintained ownership until the State of California acquired the building in 1953. (Courtesy of the Historic Italian Hall Foundation.)

One of the few remaining Eastlake Victorian structures in Los Angeles, in the 1920s, the Sepulveda House on North Main Street was home to an Italian store and sausage factory owned by the Spineglio family. At Christmastime, the shop, like many Italian groceries in the area, featured traditional Italian specialties such as *panforte, panettone,* and stuffed figs. (Courtesy of El Pueblo Historical Monument.)

The Cerrina family, owners of the Cavour Restaurant, located at 425 North Los Angeles Street (present home of the Chinese American Museum), pose in front of their business, which was named after the hero of Italy's unification. (Courtesy of El Pueblo Historical Monument.)

In the old Plaza Firehouse, the site where, years earlier, the city's first Italian settler built his home, another Italian, Angelo Rabaglino (seen here in his World War I uniform), operated a saloon and lodging house. (Courtesy of Dr. William Fasoli.)

Once the Cosmopolitan Saloon, today the Plaza Firehouse is a museum of firefighting history. (Courtesy of El Pueblo Historical Monument.)

While best known for its Mexican history, even after socialite and preservationist Christine Sterling transformed Olvera Street into a Mexican-style marketplace in 1930, Italians maintained their long-owned businesses on the street. (Courtesy of El Pueblo Historical Monument.)

The Peluffo family served Italian food in their Olvera Street restaurant Casa di Pranzo until the late 1930s. After constantly being questioned, "What's an Italian restaurant doing on Olvera Street?" the Peluffos changed the restaurant's name to Café Caliente and began serving Mexican cuisine. It was among the city's most fashionable nightspots during the 1940s and 1950s, and the hospitality of owner Lena Peluffo, pictured on the menu's cover, was well known. The restaurant and nightclub was later renamed El Paseo Inn and featured floor shows and live music. It remains a popular Olvera Street restaurant. (Courtesy of the Pedrini family.)

Known for many years as the "Mayor of Olvera Street," Frank Arconti, pictured with his wife, Adele, operated a successful hardware store on Olvera Street adjacent to where he had established a fuel and feed business in 1893. His daughter Victoria worked in the store before opening Olvera Street's popular souvenir shop, Casa de Loza, which specialized in Native American crafts.

Across the old city plaza on Main Street, Paul Mance, an émigré from Bari who had shortened his name from Manciapinto, owned the Merced Theater, the oldest theater in the city built in 1870. (Author's collection.)

In the Merced, which had ceased to be a theater in 1876, Mance—pictured with his wife, Amalia, and daughter—ran the Plaza Club, a thriving saloon, and El Oyo, a billiard hall. Referred to affectionately in Barese dialect as *cavali*, or "man of honor," Mance had an inner circle of friends that included Sheriff Eugene Biscailuz. William Fasoli, Mance's son-in-law, managed the Plaza Club until the early 1950s, when the State of California purchased the Merced Theater through eminent domain. (Courtesy of Dr. William Fasoli.)

Nearly 90 percent of Italians entering California in 1900 came from an agricultural or maritime background. In Los Angeles, they had become a major force within the city's produce market, dominated the fishing industry, and owned thriving canneries, food processing and distribution plants, and packinghouses. (Courtesy of the Los Angeles Public Library, Herald Examiner Collection.)

By 1910, Italian American–owned food companies in the state of California produced an excess of $63 million annually. The humble beginnings of the numerous Italian farmers, small business owners, and produce peddlers seldom foreshadowed the empires they would create as their modest businesses evolved into companies such as Del Monte, California Poultry, Tama Trading, and Perricone Citrus. Gaetano Uddo is one of the countless Horatio Alger stories that the community contains. To support his family, Uddo left school at age nine and pedaled groceries on a horse-drawn cart.

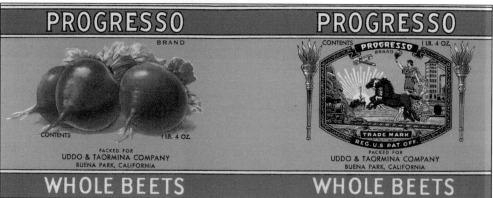

Following World War I, Uddo and his cousin Vincent Taormina founded the Uddo Taormina Corporation, which specialized in canned foods and imported Italian products distributed under the labels Flag, Liberty, and Il Progresso. Il Progresso later became the famous Progresso brand and was the first canned, ready-to-serve soup in the United States.

Following the death of his father, Joe, 15-year-old Sicilian American Sam Perricone (center) relocated his mother and three siblings from Pueblo, Colorado, to Los Angeles, where they settled in Lincoln Heights. To support the family, Sam worked for an olive oil company during the day and, in the evenings, purchased second-grade lemons from local groves. Sleeping fewer than a handful of hours each night, the young Perricone awoke before dawn and sold the lemons at the Grand Central Market, his first step to becoming a wholesaler. (Courtesy of the Perricone family.)

By 1964, Perricone Citrus wholesaled $7 million annually to stores throughout the West and distributed nationally and to numerous countries worldwide. After purchasing extensive acreage throughout the Pacific, the Perricone Citrus empire soon expanded to include complimentary industries such as produce, trucking, and cold storage. Perricone, seen here in 1936, later purchased Luer Packing Company, the Los Angeles meatpacking house that opened in 1885, and owned Disneyland's Sunkist Citrus House. (Courtesy of the Perricone family.)

Many small business owners became legends in their industries. In 1905, Giovanni "John" Lopizich, who had achieved considerable success as a pharmacist, established the International Savings and Exchange Bank. The International Savings and Exchange Bank and Bank of Italy played integral roles in the city's economic development, loaning businesses the capital necessary for their growth. While Bank of Italy was later purchased by Bank of America, the 1921 building still stands at 505 West Seventh Street and is a city landmark. (Courtesy of the Los Angeles Public Library, Security Pacific Bank Collection.)

One of the leading automobile dealerships in Southern California today, Bozzani Motors began in 1912 as a modest bicycle shop located at 632 North Main Street. An advance in capital allowed brothers Amerigo, Joe, and Carlo Bozzani to open a showroom selling Overland and Willys-Knight automobiles. (Courtesy of the Historic Italian Hall Foundation.)

The Bozzanis' dealership on North Broadway sold 2,200 automobiles in 1928 alone. (Courtesy of the Historic Italian Hall Foundation.)

Amerigo Bozzani (fifth from right) would later become a California Highway Commissioner who oversaw the construction of the state's first freeway, the Arroyo Seco Parkway. (Courtesy of the Los Angeles Public Library.)

Simone and Domenico Meaglia (left) immigrated to the United States from Bosconero, Italy, in 1912. On Little Italy's Date Street, which no longer exists today, the brothers established the American Foundry, which manufactured the pipes that continue to run through many parts of the city and provided employment to thousands of newly arrived immigrants.

Commissioned to build the workers' quarters at the Guasti Winery, Pietro and Emil Pozzo (right), natives of Brusnengo, Piedmont, established a construction company in Los Angeles.

Within 15 years, the Pozzo Construction Company, which employed countless Italians, had built over 300 buildings in the city, including the French Hospital (now Pacific Alliance Medical Center), two of the earliest buildings at UCLA, Shriners Hospital, the former Van de Kamp's factory, and the West Coast headquarters for the National Biscuit Company (Nabisco), now the fashionable Biscuit Lofts. (Courtesy of the Los Angeles Public Library, Herald Examiner Collection.)

In the late 1800s, wealthy tobacco mogul Abbot Kinney dreamed of establishing a resort town culturally reminiscent of Venice, Italy, complete with canals, gondolas, amusement parks, hotel resorts, and Venetian-style buildings on the oceanfront property south of Santa Monica. Carlo Marchetti (right) helped Kinney realize his vision, providing Kinney with technical and artistic counsel responsible for Venice's authenticity.

In 1905, Marchetti became the proprietor of the Ship Café, located alongside Venice's Abbott Kinney Pier. Fashioned after a Spanish galleon, the hotel restaurant offered haute cuisine served by staff dressed as 16th-century naval officers. Catering to a well-heeled clientele, the Ship hosted some of the most opulent parties of the era, attended by Hollywood elite the likes of Buster Keaton and Rudolph Valentino. The evening before Prohibition took effect, upwards of 100,000 revelers flooded the resort, paying $300 to secure a table. (Courtesy of the Los Angeles Public Library, Herald Examiner Collection.)

The degree to which Los Angeles afforded Italians the potential for upward mobility became ever apparent in the early 1900s, as members of *La Colonia* rose to positions of prominence in business, academics, and politics. Joseph Marchetti, the son of Carlo Marchetti, became a prominent litigator and Los Angeles Superior Court justice. Practicing at the Queen of Angels and French Hospital, Dr. Francesco Bonura (left), originally from Contessa Entellina, Sicily, was "the" Italian colony's physician from 1920 to 1950. He also conducted the medical examination required for admittance to the Garibaldina Society.

A graduate of Columbia University and Southwestern Law School, Los Angeles Superior Court judge Alfred Paonessa was California's first Italian to receive the governor's judicial nomination. Following World War II when the city witnessed a resurgence in Ku Klux Klan activity, the beloved judge delivered a major blow to the Klan, limiting its ability to organize since it "taught social hatred through violence."

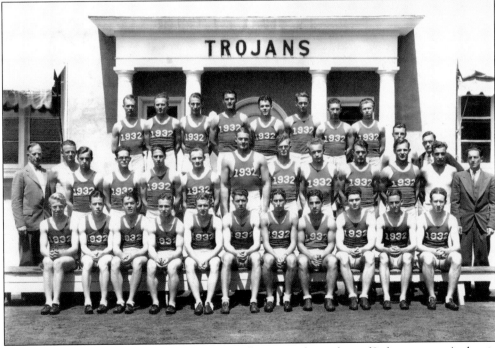

The academic excellence and athletic talent of Albert Vignolo, nephew of Italian pioneer Ambrosio Vignolo, led him to the University of Southern California, where he studied business and was a member of the track team. He is pictured in the second row, fifth from the right. A shareholder of the Italian Vineyard Company, upon graduation Vignolo managed his family's business, the Vignolo Corporation, which, established in 1865, specialized in imported foods, wines, and liquors. (Courtesy of the Historic Italian Hall Foundation.)

As educators, activists, businesspeople, artists, mothers, and anchors of the family, Italian women were inextricably connected to every aspect of the community and played an integral role in its success. Equal partners in family-owned businesses, Italian American women yielded considerable social and economic power. Through charitable organizations including the Italian Women's Club, Italian American women such as Isabella Vignolo assisted the needy and supported educational programs. Vignolo taught English to immigrant children at Castelar Street Elementary School and organized the first classes for non-English-speaking students offered by the Los Angeles Board of Education. Her tireless work with the Italian Red Cross led her to win the silver medal from the Italian government in 1920. (Courtesy of the Historic Italian Hall Foundation.)

As early as 1905, the Italian colony organized protests against proposed no-saloon ordinances, stating that such legislation amounted to an abridgement of personal liberty and posed a hardship to those engaged in viticulture. The passage of Prohibition in 1920 devastated the wine industry and forced most wineries to close. This 1927 photograph depicts authorities disposing of $150,000 worth of spirits confiscated during the Christmas holiday. (Courtesy of the Los Angeles Public Library, Herald Examiner Collection.)

A handful of vintners, including Santo Cambianca, who had established a winery in Lincoln Heights in 1917, survived by manufacturing grape juice and sacramental and medicinal wines. Today Cambianca's winery, the San Antonio Winery, is the oldest winery in the city. Other wineries, in spite of Prohibition, sold "wine bricks" or grape concentrate, which was legal and essential to produce wine for home consumption or bootlegging. Giacomo and Giovanni Vai, who owned the North Cucamonga Winery, launched an extensive promotional campaign for their Padre's Wine Elixir Tonic and Padre's Bitter Wine. The tonics, they pledged, would be recommended without hesitation by health professionals. (Courtesy of the Historic Italian Hall Foundation.)

Giacomo Vai e l'automobile "reclame"

In addition to causing economic ruin to the community, Prohibition proved a failed experiment in Los Angeles as it had elsewhere in the country, fueling violence, corruption, and organized crime. (Courtesy of the *Los Angeles Times*.)

Sam Matranga, whose murder is profiled on the previous page, was killed in his front yard, pictured here, at 1837 Darwin Avenue in Lincoln Heights when four men in a green car shot three rounds at him. The police considered his killing one among a series of murders associated with Black Hand extortion. (Author's collection.)

Dominick De Soto, standing in a police lineup, was a suspect in the murder of August Palumbo, an alleged bootlegger who was shot to death in his automobile. Palumbo was the seventh bootlegger to be killed in a six-week period during 1928. (Courtesy of the Los Angeles Public Library, Herald Examiner Collection.)

Pictured here with attorney W. T. Kendrick Jr. (left) are
Vito Ardito (center) and Mike Pupillo, who were also
arrested for the murder of Palumbo. The two men were
later released for lack of evidence. (Courtesy of the Los
Angeles Public Library, Herald Examiner Collection.)

While the *Los Angeles Times* had previously treated the Italian
community with high regard, during the 1920s, the newspaper
described Italians in increasingly racial, unflattering terms. It
reported on the violence of the "Sicilian colony" and contended
that Italians represented "the ills of immigration" and contributed
to the "decline in the wages and the standard of [living] in the
American worker." To the delight of sensationalistic journalists,
Prohibition was linked to a string of murders, many of which
remain unsolved to this day. (Courtesy of the *Los Angeles Times*.)

67

The disappearance of Anthony Buccola, pictured at his wedding in chapter five (p. 106), was thought to have been linked to that of wealthy wine merchant Frank Baumgarteker, for whose case Buccola was considered a would-be informant. (Courtesy of the *Los Angeles Times*.)

Vineyardist Joseph Ardizzone, along with Jack Dragna and John Lopizich, served on the board of the Italian Protective League, which, chaired by California state senator Joseph Pedrotti, campaigned against the Wright Liquor Enforcement Act (the California State Dry Act). Ardizzone owned a ranch in Sunland and a home in Lincoln Heights at 241 South Avenue Eighteen, pictured here. Before his disappearance, Ardizzone had been wounded when gunmen shot and killed his associate Jimmy Basile. (Author's collection.)

Four

RELIGION AND CULTURE

A myriad of forces shaped the lives of Italian Angelenos in the early 20th century. At the local level, envisioning Los Angeles as a center of "Anglo-Saxonism," policy makers and the city's elite sought the assistance of settlement houses to assimilate immigrants and the urban poor. In the national arena, fears of competition from foreign workers, social philosophies such as eugenics, and the desire to maintain the country's ethnic status quo, led Congress to pass the Quota Act of 1921 and the more restrictive Immigration Act of 1924. The laws limited Southern and Eastern European immigration and barred immigration from the Asia-Pacific Triangle entirely. Between 1900 and 1910, an average of 200,000 Italians entered the United States annually. The Immigration Act of 1924 curtailed this number to 4,000 per year.

Hollywood also influenced the public's attitudes and conceptions of Italians and, in turn, Italians' self-perception and interaction with the dominant culture. Since the earliest days of motion pictures, Hollywood vilified Italians, depicted them as uneducated working-class buffoons, violent mobsters, anarchists, bimbos, and nymphs. Films such as *Black Hand* (1906), *Italian Blood* (1911), *Last of the Mafia* (1915), and *The Italian* (1915, originally titled *The Dago*) made Italian synonymous with organized crime. Work for Italian actors was limited to inconsequential, cartoonish parts, while directors usually selected Anglo actors to play the roles of Italians and other marginalized groups. The relationship between Hollywood, the nation, and Italians contains numerous contradictions. In the same years that Sacco and Vanzetti were executed for the threat they represented in what is regarded as possibly the greatest miscarriage of justice in American history, Hollywood exulted the foreignness and forbidden eroticism of another Italian, the original "Latin lover," Rudolph Valentino. While the country celebrated Italian art and architecture, it did so in absence of Italians.

Not all Italians accepted the attacks against them passively, however. Pietro Gandolfo, chairman of the Los Angeles Sacco-Vanzetti Defense Committee, organized demonstrations against the executions, an act that led to his later arrest. In San Pedro, longshoreman Archie "Jumbo" Real (Achille Reali) agitated for workers' rights to organize, laying the foundation for the worker's movement and historic strikes of the years to come. Non-Italians also rallied the cause. In 1913, International Workers of the World labor agitator-lyricist Joe Hill was arrested for lending musical support to striking Italian dockworkers.

La Dante Alighieri
Los Angeles April 13th 1908

While the gangster myth and the ever-growing emphasis placed on "Americanism" prompted an untold number of Italian Americans to distance themselves from their culture, adopt anglicized names, and cease to speak their mother tongue, many Italians remained proudly attached to their *italianitá*. Through its promotion of Italian culture and Italian language instruction, groups such as the Dante Alighieri Society ensured that Italian expatriates did not forget their origins. (Courtesy of the Historic Italian Hall Foundation.)

The Dante Alighieri Society also hosted dignitaries such as Ernesto Nathan, the progressive mayor of Rome. The society was one of the city's many Italian charitable, political, educational, social, fraternal, and religious organizations that formed in the 1900s. Other organizations included the Mazzini Club and Societá Vittorio Emanuele (named after the hero of the Risorgimento and in honor of the first king of united Italy, respectively), St. Peter's Society (a religious group), Societá Soccorso (a self-help society), Ex-Combattenti Italiani (a veteran's group), Il Circolo Operaio Italiano (the Italian Worker's Club), and Club Schermistico (a fencing club). (Courtesy of the Historic Italian Hall Foundation.)

Members of the Italian Cycling Club of Los Angeles included Carlo (8) and Joe (7) Bozzani and Frank Longo (6), who, similar to the Bozzani brothers, would establish a successful automobile dealership in Los Angeles that remains one of the leading in the industry today. (Courtesy of the Historic Italian Hall Foundation.)

In 1905, prominent members of the Italian colony established the Italian Relief Committee. Initially, the group's focus was to assist indigent Italians of Los Angeles; however, after earthquakes struck San Francisco in 1907 and Messina, Sicily, in 1909, the Italian Relief Committee expanded its focus to support paesani in the devastated regions. The committee's benefit events generated over $18,000 to aid the stricken. By 1914, the Italian Relief Committee directed its efforts to the community as a whole, donating generously to Children's Hospital and a myriad of other charitable causes. (Courtesy of the *Los Angeles Times*.)

Italian organizations frequently sponsored weekend picnics at the Pelanconi Ranch in the present-day city of Glendale, Arroyo Seco Park in northeast Los Angeles, Casserini Ranch in Santa Monica, Hazard Park in East Los Angeles, and at local beaches. Hay-filled wagons usually collected attendees at the Italian Hall on North Main Street. At picnics such as this one, held at Griffith Park in the 1920s, attendees competed in *il tiro del formaggio*, or the hurling of a 25-pound round of cheese. (Courtesy of Elda Maga Pilj.)

The Societá Bosconerese, an organization comprised of immigrants and their descendants from the Piedmontese town of Bosconero, hosted multi-generational dances at the Italian Club located at 676 San Fernando Street and the original parish hall at St. Peter's Church. (Courtesy of Mary Mesarotti Oliver.)

Members of the Pugliese lodge of the Order of Sons of Italy in America pose for the baptism of the American and Italian flags in 1926. Puglia is a region in southeastern Italy. Significant numbers of Pugliese from the towns of Canneto, Bitritto, and Madrone, Bari, settled in Los Angeles. On the right of the banner are Lorenzo Nicassio (left) and Michael Addante. Costanza Addante Fiore is the young girl seated on the right; Maria LaBianca is the young girl seated on the left. (Courtesy of Mary Billi.)

In the late 1800s, the exodus from the small Sicilian town of Contessa Entellina, located in the Province of Palermo and district of Corleone, was so great that more Contessioti lived in the United States than in the village. The Contessa Entellina Society, seen here picnicking in Griffith Park, claimed over 200 members. (Courtesy of the Historic Italian Hall Foundation.)

In the 1920s, Sicilians from Piana dei Greci formed the Giorgio Kastriota Club, which met in a hall on Castelar and Alpine Streets. The organization derives its name from the leader of the resistance movement against the Turkish occupation of Albania in 1421. (Courtesy of James Griffin.)

In 1904, Los Angeles bishop Thomas Conaty, concerned about the religious welfare of Italian Catholics in Los Angeles, ordered the creation of two churches, St. Peter's and Immaculate Conception. St. Peter's Italian Church, still in existence, began as a small frame structure on San Fernando Street (now North Spring Street). There Bishop Conaty appointed Fr. Tito Piacentini "to produce good Catholics according to Italian tradition." Eleven years later, the church moved to its present site at 1039 North Broadway, the grounds of the old Calvary Cemetery. St. Peter's occupied the former cemetery memorial chapel (erected in 1890) of Andres Briswalter, a wealthy Angeleno. (Courtesy of St. Peter's Italian Church.)

| | Los Angeles, California, _thirtieth_ of _August_ A.D. _1904_. After complying with all canonical and legal regulations, on this day the Rev. _Titus Piacentini_ joined in Marriage Mr. _Domenico Palliassotti_, aged _25 years_ native of _Italy_, resident of _Los Angeles_ and _Maddalena Aiasso_, aged _18 years_, native of _Italy_, resident of _Los Angeles_ The witnesses _Frank Palliassotti_ and _Signora Aiasso_ — |

Palliassotti Aiasso

August 1904

1

In witness I sign, *Piacentini* Rector.

Cecchini Giambastiani

Los Angeles, California, _21st_ of _August_ A.D. _1904_. After complying with all canonical and legal regulations, on this day the Rev. _Titus Piacentini_ joined in marriage Mr. _Ottavio Cecchini_, aged _24 years_ native of _Italy_, resident of _Los Angeles_ and _Noemi Giambastiani_ aged _18 years_, native of _Italy_, resident of _Los Angeles_ The witnesses _Antonio Cecchini, Adele Fazzi_

2

In witness I sign, *Piacentini* Rector.

Turiace Santo

Los Angeles, California, _4th_ of _Septemb._ A.D. _1904_. After complying with all canonical and legal regulations, on this day the Rev. _Titus Piacentini_ joined in Marriage Mr. _Pasquale Turiace_, aged _22 years_ native of _Italy_, resident of _Los Angeles_ and _Teresa Santo_, aged _17_, native of _Italy_, resident of _Los Angeles_ The witnesses _John Lopizich Marianna Lopizich_

September 1904

3

In witness I sign, *Piacentini* Rector.

Sobue De Salvo

Los Angeles, California, _11th_ of _September_ A.D. _1904_. After complying with all canonical and legal regulations, on this day the Rev. _Titus Piacentini_ joined in marriage Mr. _Georgio Sobue_, aged _23_ native of _Italy_, resident of _Los Angeles_ and _Rosa De Salvo_ aged _23_, native of _Italy_, resident of _Los Angeles_ The witnesses _Santo Onofrio, Concetta Onofrio_

4

In witness I sign, *Piacentini* Rector.

The first couple married at St. Peter's Church was Domenico Pagliassotti and Maddalena Aiasso on August 30, 1904. Antonio Zaro was the first child baptized at St. Peter's in September of the same year. (Courtesy of St. Peter's Italian Church.)

Parishioners created religious societies to preserve the celebrations and honor the patron saint or Madonna of the province from where the immigrants originated. Both solemn and joyful, feast day celebrations for San Vittoriano, Madonna delle Stelle, and other saints featured elaborate processions, traditional food, and music and often lasted several days. (Courtesy of St. Peter's Italian Church.)

Saints' statues, adorned with rich fabrics, money, and other offerings, were placed on platforms and carried several blocks. (Courtesy of Dr. William Fasoli.)

Proud recipients of their First Communion pose with Fr. Julian Uriarte on the steps of St. Peter's Church around 1930. (Courtesy of St. Peter's Church.)

For the purposes of celebrating or grieving and in search of the familiar devotions and culture of their homeland, Italians from all parts of the city called St. Peter's their parish. (Courtesy of Dr. William Fasoli.)

Date	Names	Officiant	Birth / Baptism Information	Notes
			Born in Los Angeles - April 14 - 1896 Baptized in St. Joseph's Church	
April 18 - 1914	Mr. & Mrs. Costantino Orlandi	Rev. B.J. Schiaparelli	Born Decemb. 13 - 1886 in ?? prov. Genova Circ. Chiavaro baptized alla parrocchia di ??	Disp. from 3 publ. of banns
			Born November 30 - 1891 in San Francisco Cal. baptized at the Church of St. Peter and Paul (Italian)	
April 19 - 1914	Arthur Rinaldi - Josie Della Chiara	Rev. B.J. Schiaparelli	Born May 14 - 1888 in Rocca di Mezzo prov. Aquila baptized in Rocca di Mezzo	disp. from 3 publ. of banns
			Born July 4 - 1889 in Rocca di Mezzo Aquila baptized in Rocca di Mezzo	
April 26 - 1914	Philip Mandala - Rose Mandala	Rev. B.J. Schiaparelli	Born Novem. 2 - 1879 in Piana dei Greci prov. Palermo baptized in Piana dei Greci	Vita Mamola a widow of the late Matranga Giuseppe
			Born Sept. 8 - 1885 in Piana dei Greci prov. Palermo baptized in Piana dei Greci	
June 6 - 1914	Nicola (Nick) Lobue - Aida Fehlhaber	Rev. B.J. Schiaparelli	Born March 23 - 1894 in Piana dei Greci prov. Palermo baptized alla matrice di San Demetrio 1634	
			Born May 7 - 1896 in Nebraska - a Methodist convert, baptized conditionally June 5 - 1914 at the Immac. Concept. Church dispen. Baptisms page 23	
July 19 - 1914	Salvatore Spera - Lucia Di Carlo	Rev. B.J. Schiaparelli	Born January 21 - 1889 in Bagheria prov. Palermo baptized alla matrice di Millici prov. Palermo	
			Born Octob 27 - 1897 in Pattersonville Louisiana baptized in Pattersonville - Louisiana	
July 26 - 1914	Pietro Locascio - Bertha Provenzano	Rev. B.J. Schiaparelli	Born March 24 - 1891 in Piana dei Greci Palermo baptized in San Demetrio Piana dei Greci	
			Born in Franklyn - Louisiana August 17 - 1897	
August 2nd - 1914	Luigi Benice - Susanna Benice	Rev. B.J. Schiaparelli	Born January 1st 1884 in Paradela prov. Lugo - España	
			Born March 6 - 1886 in Palermo, Sicily Parrocchia di San Giuseppe Paler.	
September 6 - 1914	Paul Bruscia - Vita Camarga	Rev. B.J. Schiaparelli	Born in Piana dei Greci prov. Palermo April 12 - 1893 Baptized in Piana dei Greci (Chiesa Greca)	
			Born in Morgan City Louisiana June 4 - 1898 Baptized in Morgan City	
September 6 - 1914	Angelo Cirino - Loretta Spera	Rev. B.J. Schiaparelli	Born in Corleone, prov. Palermo May 1 - 1888 baptized dalla matrice di Corleone	
			Born in Trinidad Colorado April 6 - 1896 baptized in Trinidad, Colorado	

The second church, Immaculate Conception, was located on Fourteenth and Wilson Streets in the city's Sicilian enclave. While Immaculate Conception's baptismal, marriage, and death records have been preserved, little other information is known about the church. It seems that in 1924, Immaculate Conception relocated to Avenue Twenty and Darwin Avenue in Lincoln Heights. Inspection of the church's marriage records reveals that many of the parishioners hailed from Piana dei Greci, Corleone, and other villages in the province of Palermo, Sicily.

Today the church is called Our Lady Help of Christians and serves a predominantly Spanish-speaking congregation. (Courtesy of the Los Angeles Public Library.)

Prior to the construction of St. Peter's and Immaculate Conception, Italians attended the Plaza Church on North Main Street. The marriage of Clare Coffey and Victor Vincent Valla, a descendant of the Pelanconi-Tononi families, was one of many marriages that took at the Plaza Church even after the construction of the two Italian parishes. (Courtesy of Anthony Valla.)

Other couples, such as Jack Bonura and Bessie Palermo, exchanged their vows at Sacred Heart Church in Lincoln Heights. (Courtesy of Linda Marcus.)

To this day, Sacred Heart's stained-glass windows bear the names of the church's Italian benefactors. (Courtesy of the Los Angeles Public Library.)

Numerous missions and settlement houses provided assistance to immigrants. Though overwhelmingly Catholic, some Italians belonged to other religious denominations. At the Italian Baptist Church at 2021 Mozart Street in Lincoln Heights, Pastors Henry Re and G. W. Romano conducted services in Italian and English. Reverend Malinverni of the United Italian Presbyterian Mission located at 522 Alpine Street provided food, clothing, and general assistance to needy parishioners. Rev. Bruno Bruni's congregation at the Wilson Street Methodist Episcopal Chapel included 200 Italians. The chapel offered sewing classes to young women and English-language classes. (Courtesy of the Historic Italian Hall Foundation.)

In 1918, Pastor G. Bromley Oxnam founded the Church of All Nations under the auspices of the Methodist Church. Located in Boyle Heights, it was the largest and most effective social welfare organization in Los Angeles, drawing a multiethnic community of thousands, including a significant number of Italians, to its social welfare programs and Sunday services. (Courtesy of the Los Angeles Public Library.)

A project of the Immigrant Welfare Bureau of Associated Catholic Charities, the Santa Rita Settlement House, located on North Main Street in Dogtown, offered recreational activities, religious instruction, and medical care to hundreds of members of the local Mexican and Italian community, including, from left to right, Artiglia Munge and sisters Mary and Eda DeMaio. (Courtesy of Mary Wallace and Eda Tortomasi.)

Viewing education as a means of social change, settlement houses such as Santa Rita promoted English-language acquisition and taught Anglo middle-class values. (Courtesy of Mary Wallace and Eda Tortomasi.)

The Plaza Methodist Church, located near Macy Street (present-day Cesar Chavez Avenue) assisted Italian and Mexican immigrants. (Courtesy of the Plaza United Methodist Church.)

The Los Angeles Playground movement began in 1904 with the aim of promoting middle-class values and providing young people with a supervised alternative to street life. The first public park created especially for children was the Violet Street Playground, located in the Seventh Ward between Atlantic, Seventh, Violet, and Mateo Streets in the heart of the Sicilian enclave. (Courtesy of the Los Angeles Public Library.)

The 2-acre site offered open fields, play equipment, clubhouses, a gymnasium, and a variety of organized athletic and arts programs. (Courtesy of the Los Angeles Public Library.)

To provide for the spiritual well-being of the community, Bishop Conaty recruited Mother Francis Xavier Cabrini. Cabrini, who became the first U.S. citizen to be canonized a saint, established the Regina Coeli Orphanage on North Hill Street. She provided childcare and religious education to the largely Italian and Mexican community, acts that led her to be named the "patron saint" of immigrants. In 1906, after observing the propensity of the economically disadvantaged to contract diseases such as tuberculosis, she founded the Mother Cabrini Preventorium in Burbank. (Courtesy of Missionary Sisters of the Sacred Heart, St. Frances Cabrini.)

In 1924, Los Angeles, the city of modernity and progress, was struck by an ancient disease—an outbreak of the pneumonic and bubonic plague, the last of its kind in the urban United States, which took the lives of 33 people and prompted a quarantine of five city districts. The first case was traced to a boardinghouse at 742 Clara Street in the Eighth Ward. Within days, most of the boarders and those who came into contact with them succumbed to the disease. The majority of the victims were impoverished Mexicans; however, Italian immigrant Joe Bagnola was among the casualties. (Courtesy of the Bancroft Library, University of California, Berkeley.)

Calvary Cemetery relocated to its present-day East Los Angeles location in 1896. For generations, Calvary has been the resting place of Angelenos of various ethnicities, including significant numbers of Italians. (Author's collection.)

Gabriello Spini founded *L'Italo Americano* newspaper in 1908 as a competitor for *L'Eco della Colonia.* Located in Little Italy on San Fernando Street, at first, every issue was composed painstakingly by hand by placing one metal character at a time on a metal plate that was then carried to the printer. (Courtesy of *L'Italo Americano.*)

Published today by philanthropist Robert Barb*L'Italo Americano* celebrated its centennial in 2008 and continues to be the voice of the Southern California Italian community. (Courtesy of *L'Italo Americano.*)

Italian households in Los Angeles were typically multigenerational and included extended family members. Sunday afternoons were reserved as family time and culminated with a large dinner, often attended by dozens of family members, neighbors, and kin. (Courtesy of Elda Maga Pilj.)

For many Italian families, including the Romanos and Troncallis of Lincoln Heights, winemaking was a cherished tradition in which everyone participated. (Courtesy of Josephine Romano Lyden.)

By the 1920s, the city's Italian youth partook in many of the same activities as their Anglo counterparts, attended "shows" and dances, enjoyed jazz, and donned fashionable attire. Most Italian families did not permit their daughters to date without chaperones, however. (Courtesy of Elda Maga Pilj.)

Military service was one way in which immigrants demonstrated their commitment to the principles of American democracy. Shortly after his arrival, Louis Castellano joined the U.S. Army and participated in World War I. Italians have served in the U.S. military in every war since the American Revolution. (Courtesy of Elda Maga Pilj.)

Like many immigrants, Italians recognized that their success in the United States rested upon their ability to master the English language. Italians frequently enrolled in evening English-language instruction courses at adult schools such as McKinley Avenue. (Courtesy of Elda Maga Pilj.)

Fidel La Barba
CHAMPION

Discovered at age 14, Lincoln Heights' featherweight Fidel La Barba boxed at the Los Angeles Athletic Club and later won the gold medal at the 1924 Olympic Games in Paris. (Courtesy of John Nese/Galco's Old World Grocery.)

The quintessential Los Angeles writer, inspiration to Beat generation authors, and the voice of immigrant America, John Fante settled in the Bunker Hill neighborhood of Los Angeles in the late 1920s. His novels, including *Ask the Dusk* and *Dreams from Bunker Hill*, spoke of reoccurring themes such as poverty, Italian American identity, and Catholicism. (Courtesy of the Los Angeles Public Library.)

Perhaps Los Angeles's most famous grassroots artist, Sabato (or Sam or Simon) Rodia was born in 1879 into a poor family in Campania, Italy, and settled in Los Angeles in 1917. In 1921, he purchased a house in Watts, a multiethnic community in South Los Angeles. Without any formal training as an artist or architect, over a 34-year period, Rodia, shown here shortly before his death, worked daily on a collection of 17 interconnected structures that would later be known as the Watts Towers until abandoning them unexpectedly in 1955. (Courtesy of the Los Angeles Public Library, Herald Examiner Collection.)

Rodia constructed his steel towers working alone and decorated them with salvaged objects, including porcelain and ceramic tile, glass, bed frames, bottle caps, and seashells. He baptized the towers with a Spanish name, *Nuestro Pueblo*, meaning "Our Town." Today the Watts Towers are a local and national landmark. (Courtesy of Kenneth Scambray.)

By the 1920s, the city boasted countless delis and eateries that would achieve legendary status among Angelenos, including Little Joe's, the Italian Kitchen, Sformento's, Costa Grill, Sarno's, Fazzi's, Musso and Frank's, Dario's, and Piuma's Grocery. (Courtesy of the Historic Italian Hall Foundation.)

Located on the corner of Macy (present-day Cesar Chavez Avenue) and North Main Streets, one-time Italian consular agent to Los Angeles Giovanni Piuma operated a grocery and pharmacy. (Courtesy of the Historic Italian Hall Foundation.)

Angelenos recall Piuma's delectable aromas with great nostalgia. Piuma's was demolished in the 1960s to build a parking lot. (Courtesy of the Historic Italian Hall Foundation.)

Baritone Burt Rovere's Paris Inn was located on Market Street, the site of present-day Los Angeles City Hall. (Courtesy of the Los Angeles Public Library, Herald Examiner Collection.)

The Paris Inn's singing waiters delighted patrons. (Courtesy of the Los Angeles Public Library, Herald Examiner Collection.)

The long-shuttered Little's Joe's Restaurant began in 1897 as the Italian American Grocery Store. Owned by the Nuccio family, it was located on Fifth and Hewitt Streets in what is today the Arts District. (Courtesy of the Nuccio family.)

The business relocated to North Broadway and College Street in 1927 and changed its name to Little Joe's in the 1940s to avoid the wartime stigmas associated with being Italian. (Courtesy of the Nuccio family.)

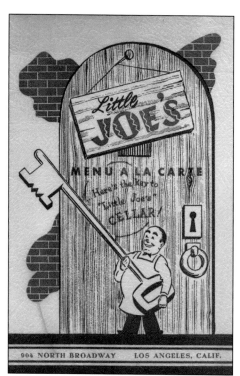

Little Joe's, a Los Angeles favorite for over 100 years, closed its doors in 1998. (Courtesy of George and Gloria Carone.)

The Italian Kitchen was located on Los Angeles and Commercial Streets, just north of the federal courthouse. It was demolished upon the construction of the Hollywood Freeway. (Courtesy of the Los Angeles Public Library, Herald Examiner Collection.)

Costa Pasta began as a small, family-owned business in the city's Sicilian enclave that made pasta by hand for local restaurants. In 2001, their annual sales exceeded 20 million pounds. (Courtesy of Connie Costa Foster.)

Most of the Italian delicatessens and grocery stores that once operated in the downtown area have disappeared, including the Gianduia Grocery Store, which was located on North Main Street in Lincoln Heights. Pictured from left to right are Maria and Pietro Gamerro and Joe Peracchino. (Courtesy of Ralph and Teresa Thompson.)

Founded in the 1920s, Eastside Market began as a grocery store that specialized in Italian meats owned by Domenico Pontrelli. By 1939, the store was too small to accommodate the business and was sold to Johnny and Frank Angiuli, who converted it into a deli. (Courtesy of the Angiuli family.)

Frank Nese, pictured above, and Gino Cortopassi operated the ever-popular Galco's Italian grocery store and deli on Castelar and Ord Streets, frequented by Samuel Goldwyn's young actors the "Dead End Kids" and the wives of Frank Sinatra and Dean Martin. It was Rocky Marciano who named the store's signature "Blockbuster" sandwich. Nese would later become partners with Al Mosca and Joe Costamagna in the Costa Grill, the venerable eatery located next door to Galco's where local dignitaries, common folk, and infamous figures including Mickey Cohen dined elbow to elbow. Galco's, located today in Highland Park, a neighborhood in northeast Los Angeles that was at one time home to a sizable Italian community, is owned and operated by Nese's son John and features over 450 varieties of soda, more than 500 beers from around the world, and dozens of old-time candies. (Courtesy of John Nese/Galco's Old World Grocery.)

Five

THE ITALIAN HALL

Recognizing the Italian community's economic viability, in 1907, Parisian-born Marie Hammel ordered the construction of a building specifically for Italian occupancy at 642–646 North Main Street, approximately two blocks north of where pioneer Giovanni Leandri had established his residence 80 years earlier. Hammel's property, located on the southeast corner of Macy Street, had been the site of the Bath Street School, the city's second public school, which had opened in 1856. In 1883, the Board of Education sold the land to Andres Briswalter who, upon his death, left the estate to business associates Isaias Hellman, cofounder of the Farmers and Merchants Bank, and Henry Hammel, Marie's husband. Marie Hammel assumed ownership of the property following her husband's death in 1904 and, soon thereafter, hired architect Julius Krause and the Pozzo Construction Company to erect a two-story yellow brick building at an estimated cost of $20,000. According to the original permits, the building's second floor was designed for use as a lodge and clubroom, while the first floor would contain four commercial businesses. The Italian Hall became the social and cultural focal point of the community, where Italian organizations met and countless events including weddings, concerts, and celebrations such as the *vendemmia*, or fall wine harvest, were held.

Non-Italians frequented the hall as well, and the building, in part because of its proximity to the Plaza, bore witness to some of the tumultuous events that shaped early-20th-century Los Angeles. Among the most hostile of all major American cities to organized labor, Los Angeles remained decidedly "open shop" for the better part of the 20th century. The *Los Angeles Times* played an active role in anti-union campaigns, rallying employers and the public behind the slogan of "industrial freedom." The Mexican and Russian Revolutions further aggravated fears of social unrest and radicalism and cemented relations between the *Times*, the Los Angeles Police Department, conservatives in local government, and the business sector. In 1909, the Los Angeles City Council issued an ordinance that prohibited free speech on city streets and private property. The Plaza received an exemption from the ban and, in the years that followed, became an important public forum for a myriad of radical factions, political exiles, revolutionaries, dissenters, and labor activists. Some of these rallies took place at the Italian Hall.

Upon the building's completion, the flags of Italy and the United States were proudly displayed on the Main Street facade's ornamental iron balcony, above which the name "Italian Hall" was emblazoned in large, gold letters. (Author's collection.)

Signs hung at the entrance announced the availability of lodge rooms and facilities for meetings, receptions, and dances. A mosaic floor with the words "Italian Hall" patterned in tile greeted visitors entering from Main Street. (Author's collection.)

In 1908, Marie Hammel, pictured here, leased the hall's upper floor to Frank Arconti, secretary of La Societá Italiana de Mutua Beneficenza (the Italian Mutual Benefit Society) to serve as the group's headquarters. (Courtesy of El Pueblo Historical Monument.)

Arconti, reclining in the first row with his hat at his side, was the president of La Societá Italiana de Mutua Beneficenza in 1898. This photograph, taken at one of the society's informal retreats in the early 1900s, captures a fraction of the group's membership. (Courtesy of the Arconti family.)

The footraces of the Garibaldina Society, often organized for charitable purposes, commenced in front of the Italian Hall. The members who participated in this race included Luigi Boldetti (far left wearing a hat), R. Nuccio (No. 11), Domenico Arobio (in back of Nuccio, wearing a hat), Ottavio Basso (No. 7, owner of Basso Bakery on Broadway and Ord Street), C. Scannavino (behind Basso, wearing a hat), A. Piantanida (at Basso's right), Gino Guasti, Domenic Merlo (No. 4), Saverino Fanetti (behind Merlo), G. Benotti (No. 3), and A. Cerrina (behind Benotti). (Courtesy of the Garibaldina Society and Maria Pia Arobio.)

The Main Street portion of the Italian Hall contained three commercial stores, including an Italian tailor's shop, a saloon, Arconti's hardware store (above), and later a billiard parlor and bicycle shop. (Courtesy of the Arconti family.)

In the early 1900s, the Italian Hall's saloon, owned by Ettore Paggi and Luigi Issoglio, was the most elegant tavern in Los Angeles. The saloon's floor bore the proprietors' surnames, arranged in tile as well as a repeating fleur de lis pattern. (Courtesy of the Paggi-Laura family.)

Ettore Paggi, pictured with his wife, Teresa Maga, and son Ettore Primo, had emigrated from Scarmagno, a small town in Piedmont, Italy. (Courtesy of the Paggi-Laura family.)

The saloon, which featured the longest bar in the city, was a favorite among the city's *prominenti*, both Italian and non-Italian. (Courtesy of the Paggi-Laura family.)

60 mo. anniversario della promulga-
zione Dello Statuto Italiano
L'ITALIAN AMERICAN CLUB
7 Giugno 1908

The large main room on the Italian Hall's second floor was spacious enough to accommodate hundreds of guests. Organizations including the Italian American Club and the Dante Alighieri Society utilized the Italian Hall for celebrations such as Italy's Republic Day and Italy's annexation of Rome. (Courtesy of the Historic Italian Hall Foundation.)

Amongst the notable visitors that the hall hosted were Umberto Nobile, the Italian aeronautical engineer, and Arctic explorer and aviator Francesco de Pinedo. (Courtesy of the Historic Italian Hall Foundation.)

Musical and theatrical performances of many genres took place at the Italian Hall, where youth of the community in particular thronged to hear Pete Pontrelli's Orchestra. Pontrelli, pictured second from the right with his early band King Tut Café, was born in Puglia, Italy, in 1898 and immigrated to the United States in 1914. In the 1920s, Pontrelli's Orchestra, which also performed at the Paris Inn and at the Red Mill on Ord Street, played Italian favorites such as "La Piemontesina" and the popular foxtrots of the time. (Courtesy of the Historic Italian Hall Foundation.)

Pontrelli's band was frequently hired to play at the numerous wedding receptions held at the Italian Hall, including that of Sicilian immigrants Anthony Buccola and Nettie Rietta in 1920. Pontrelli, whose name and saxophone are synonymous with the ballroom era in Los Angeles, entertained throughout the 1930s and 1940s at establishments such as the Palomar, the Palace, and the Figueroa Ballroom and remained in demand until the 1980s. (Courtesy of Josephine Romano Lyden.)

Il Circolo Operaio Italiano (Italian Worker's Club) frequently met at the Italian Hall. In 1917, the group organized a footrace that began in front of the Italian Hall and ended in nearby Lincoln Park. Pictured from left to right are Domenich Basso (who owned a Chrysler dealership in Little Italy on North Broadway), Frank Ghiosso, Frank Aprato, John Duretto (No. 6), Giacomo Castellano, and John Aprato. (Courtesy of David and Juliette Aprato.)

The club's exclusively male membership organized weekly Saturday evening dances at the hall and hosted banquets for important Italian holidays. (Courtesy of David and Juliette Aprato.)

Youthful and gregarious, Il Circolo Operaio Italiano acted as a unifying force in the community. Pictured here from left to right are (first row) Frank Ghiosso and John Duretto; (second row) Otto Basso, Sam Meaglia, and unidentified; (third row) Frank Aprato and "Bocchia" Denchio. (Courtesy of David and Juliette Aprato.)

Il Circolo Operaio Italiano would later merge with the Garibaldina Society. Seated in the first row, second from the left, is John Duretto. Frank Ghiosso sits with his legs outstretched (first row, third from left) and Frank Aprato with his arms folded (first row, fourth from left). Sam Meaglia is on the far right. Otto Basso is in the back row holding an accordion. John "Boccia" Denchio stands at his right. (Courtesy of David and Juliette Aprato.)

In 1919, Il Circolo Operaio Italiano held a banquet in celebration of May Day at the hall. The club likely served as the link between the Italian community and the non-Italian groups that used the hall as a site for political rallies. (Courtesy of David and Juliette Aprato.)

As the favorite gathering place for Italian and European radicals, the hall was used extensively during the Mexican Revolution by Mexican exiles and their supporters. Prominent theorists of the Mexican Revolution and founders of the Partido Liberal Mexicano (PLM), or Mexican Liberal Party, and the antigovernment paper *Regeneración*, brothers Enrique (right) and Ricardo Flores Magòn, pictured here at the Los Angeles County Jail in 1917, and the PLM met at the hall more frequently than any other Mexican revolutionary organization. (Courtesy of the *Los Angeles Times*.)

Italians participated in sociopolitical clubs with Mexicans and Anglos. One such club was El Centro de Estudios Racionales, or the Center for Rational Studies, which was headquartered on San Fernando Street. Notice of the group's meetings appeared in *Regeneración*, and they featured Spanish-, English-, Hebrew-, and Italian-speaking orators, such as Michele Fasano. The labor organization Il Gruppo 29 di Luglio (the 29th of July Group) organized a celebration at the Italian Hall in 1911. Admission for men was 25¢; women were admitted free of charge. (Courtesy of the Archivo Magòn.)

For a brief period, *Regeneración* was printed in Italian. *La Rivolta* was another locally published, radical, Italian-language newspaper. (Courtesy of the Archivo Magòn.)

An anonymous Italian immigrant once said, "They distributed leaflets in my village that said the streets in America were paved with gold. When we arrived, we found that the streets were not paved in gold. In fact, they were not paved at all. What's more, it was the job of the Dago to pave them!" In the 1920s, Southern California Italians, including Giuseppe Maga (pictured), a member of Il Circolo Operaio Italiano who would later patent an early power lawnmower, used sociopolitical clubs as a means to speak out collectively against labor discrimination and the National Origins Act. (Courtesy of Elda Maga Pilj.)

On May 16, 1912, Emma Goldman spoke to a crowd of hundreds at the Italian Hall. As joblessness in Los Angeles increased, in 1913, a coalition of Mexicans, Italians, and Anglos gathered at the Plaza. The Christmas Day Riot, as it would later be known, occurred after a struggle ensued between a member of the crowd and the police. One demonstrator was killed and another wounded. Law enforcement used the incident as justification for "cracking down," and in the days that followed, several arrests were made, including that of Silvio Luti, an Italian youth who allegedly extolled workers to exact revenge on the Los Angeles Police Department for his fellow agitator's death. (Courtesy of University of Michigan.)

The rallies held at the Italian Hall frequently drew the attention of the Los Angeles Police Department, particularly the department's infamous radical-hunting "Red Squad." Following the arrest of the Flores Magòn brothers on charges of defamation and sending indecent material in the mail, Emma Goldman returned to the Italian Hall in 1916 to raise funds for the brothers' defense. Ricardo Flores Magòn was later arrested again for distributing seditious literature at a rally held at the Italian Hall and sentenced to 20 years in prison. He died under mysterious circumstances at the U.S. Penitentiary, Leavenworth, Kansas, in 1922. (Courtesy of the *Los Angeles Times*.)

In the 1930s, the Italian community, now numbering 30,000, outgrew the building and ceased to use the hall. Urban expansion and demographic shifts, which altered Italian American residential and commercial patterns, also played a role. The Garibaldina Society moved to new quarters at 810 Castelar Street, and the Italian Hall then became the Plaza Art Center. (Courtesy of the Arconti family.)

In 1932, the center's director, F. K. Ferenz, commissioned the acclaimed Mexican muralist Davíd Alfaro Siqueiros to paint an 82-by-18-foot mural entitled *America Tropical* on the second-story south exterior wall of the building. Because of its controversial content, the mural was soon whitewashed. (Author's collection.)

In the years that followed, the second floor of the Italian Hall was used for storage, while Olvera Street stores and eateries occupied the first floor. When the historic significance of the Italian Hall became evident in 1989, luminaries of the Los Angeles Italian community, namely Joe Cerrell (at podium), Phillip Bartenetti, and Maria De Tone Cooper, organized a support group, later known as the Historic Italian Hall Foundation, to promote awareness of the hall's cultural and historical significance and to raise funds for the development of a museum. Elected officials including former Assemblymen Gil Cedillo (on the right of the podium), Antonio Villaraigosa, and Los Angeles Councilmen John Ferraro (far right) and Nick Pacheco rallied to support the group's efforts by providing hundreds of thousands of dollars in state and city grants. (Courtesy of the Historic Italian Hall Foundation.)

Approximately $2 million was raised to renovate the building, which had suffered from years of neglect, and the Italian Hall was painstakingly restored to its original splendor over a three-year period. In 2001, Los Angeles commissioner Mike Gatto (far left), councilman Nick Pacheco (far right), and members of the Historic Italian Hall Foundation (including Gloria Ricci Lothrop, Phil Bartenetti, and Rosemarie Lippman) celebrate Phase I of the Italian Hall's restoration. (Courtesy of the Historic Italian Hall Foundation.)

In 2004, a water leak forced the Italian Hall to close. Since then, the Historic Italian Hall Foundation has worked closely with the City of Los Angeles to ensure the museum's reopening. In 2008, proving himself a tireless supporter of the museum project, councilman José Huizar procured the funding necessary to repair the hall during one of the most difficult fiscal climates Los Angeles has ever experienced. The Historic Italian Hall Foundation focuses its efforts on the development of a 21st-century museum, slated to open in 2011, that will document the history of Italians in Southern California. The Italian American Museum of Los Angeles will feature temporary and permanent exhibits, a research center, and will host lectures, festivals, meetings, and community events. (Author's collection.)

Six

LOOKING FORWARD

During the post–World War II years, neither nostalgia nor tradition bound Italians to the neighborhoods in which they had first settled. Scarcely an Italian could be found in Ward Eight's Little Italy, the Plaza, and its environs. The enclave of Sicilians whose clapboard homes once sat in the shadow of the Los Angeles City Market in the Sixth and Seventh Ward met the wrath of the bulldozer and were replaced by industrial warehouses. Redevelopment of the city's Old Chinatown, which centered on Alameda and Arcadia Streets adjacent to Union Station, led to the creation of New Chinatown along North Broadway in what was once the heart of the Italian enclave. Prosperous and mobile, Italians dispersed from the old neighborhoods and resettled throughout the city, establishing small clusters in Eagle Rock, Los Feliz, Highland Park, San Marino, Burbank, Encino, and Echo Park. San Pedro's Italian community, meanwhile, retained its ethnic density, comprising the only enclave that could be accurately referred to as "Little Italy." Once in the suburbs, second- and third-generation Italians adopted middle-class values, married non-Italians, and assimilated into the larger plural society. Membership to regional and devotional organizations decreased, as did the sense of connectivity to the parent culture.

This is not to say that the sense of Italian identity and community diminished entirely. The 1960s witnessed a rebirth of community life, largely attributed to Fr. Luigi Donanzan, pastor of St. Peter's Church from 1962 to 1979, who launched the Italian radio program *Ora Cattolica Italiana*, rejuvenated *L'Italo Americano* newspaper, and energized Southern California's Italians, including members of the entertainment industry, raising the capital needed for the construction of a new parish hall for St. Peter's Church, the Casa Italiana, and the retirement home Villa Scalabrini. A new generation of activists subsequently emerged, many of whom currently comprise the leaders of the nation's fifth-largest Italian community.

DON'T SPEAK THE ENEMY'S LANGUAGE!

The Four Freedoms Are Not In His Vocabulary

SPEAK AMERICAN!

Shortly after the United States declared war on Italy in 1941, the federal government classified more than 600,000 Italians living in the United States as "enemy aliens." From February through October 1942, as enemy aliens, Italians were required to register at their local post office, carry identification cards, and report all changes in employment and residence. (Courtesy of the Los Angeles Public Library, Herald Examiner Collection.)

They were prohibited from traveling a greater distance than 5 miles from their homes, were subject to curfews, and were forbidden to own guns, cameras, and short-wave radios. The restrictions led many Italians to lose their jobs and limited the freedom of movement of thousands of others. A San Francisco fisherman named Giuseppe DiMaggio could not visit the restaurant owned by his son, Joe DiMaggio. (Courtesy of the American Italian Historical Association Western Regional Chapter.)

In the same years that the surnames of the mayors of America's largest cities included La Guardia (New York) and Rossi (San Francisco), more than 100 U.S. citizens of Italian birth were forced to relocate from the East and West Coasts and the Gulf of Mexico to "safe" inland zones, while the Immigration and Naturalization Service held nearly 3,300 Italians in internment camps for varying lengths of time during the war. (Courtesy of the Los Angeles Public Library, Herald Examiner Collection.)

Though an estimated 1.2 million Americans of Italian descent served valiantly in the U.S. military, constituting one of the largest and most decorated segments of the country's combat forces of about 12 million, Italian "enemy alien" families were barred from visiting their sons at the bases where they were stationed. Lincoln Heights resident Joe Romano, the American-born son of parents who were not yet U.S. citizens, succumbed to injuries sustained in battle shortly after his return from the war. (Courtesy of Josephine Romano Lyden.)

As population expansion following World War II altered Italian Angelenos' residential patterns, postwar arrivals infused vitality into the community. Immigrants, especially from the region of Puglia, founded a host of religious and cultural organizations that served to revive Italian tradition in Los Angeles from its slumber. The newcomers also joined groups with historic ties to the community, such as the Italian Women's Club and the Garibaldina Society. (Courtesy of St. Peter's Italian Church.)

As pastor of St. Peter's Church, Fr. Luigi Donanzan (pictured fifth from left) initiated an intense, multifaceted campaign aimed at re-establishing St. Peter's as the center of Italian activity in Southern California. (Courtesy of St. Peter's Italian Church.)

A believer in the power of communication and promotion, Father Luigi, as he was affectionately known, circulated a monthly newsletter highlighting the church's activities and programs and organized an annual Italian festival at the Hollywood Palladium. (Courtesy of St. Peter's Italian Church.)

Today St. Peter's Italian Church remains the religious focal point of Italians in Los Angeles and the site of numerous cultural and religious celebrations annually, including the Feast of St. Joseph in March. (Courtesy of St. Peter's Italian Church.)

The Italians of Los Angeles continued to achieve unparalleled success in the fields of politics, business, academics, the arts, and of course, Hollywood. Beloved Los Angeles city councilman John Ferraro's 35-year tenure on council is the longest of any member. Today the community draws inspiration from local elected officials such as assemblyman Anthony Portantino and the city of Hawthorne's Mayor Larry Guidi. (Courtesy of the Historic Italian Hall Foundation.)

Legendary political consultant Joe Cerrell, pictured here, founded Cerrell and Associates, one of the nation's largest public relations firms, in 1966. During his career, which spans over five decades, Cerrell played an integral role in the presidential campaigns of John F. Kennedy, Lyndon B. Johnson, Hubert H. Humphrey, Lloyd Bentsen, John Glenn, and Al Gore. As vice chairman and immediate past president of the National Italian American Foundation, Cerrell has been a tireless advocate for all things Italian on both the local and national level. (Author's collection.)

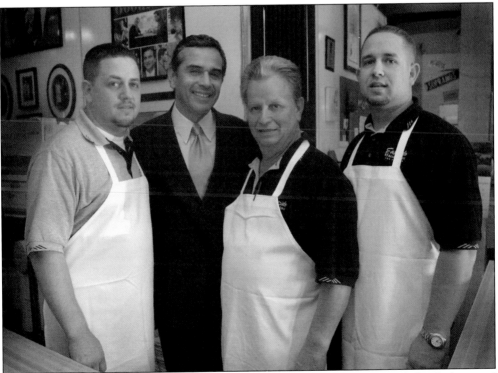

The Eastside Market, established in the 1920s and owned today by the Angiuli family (pictured with Los Angeles mayor Antonio Villaraigosa), is the last existing Italian eatery in the original enclave, located on Alpine Street. The lunchtime queue that wraps around Eastside Market testifies to the enduring popularity of the establishment's signature sandwiches, such as the "D.A. Special." (Courtesy of Gil Ortiz.)

Simply Fresh and Perricone Juice, subsidiaries of the company that Sam Perricone founded in the back of a Ford pickup truck, continue to thrive today, with three generations of the Perricone family contributing to the family business. (Courtesy of the Perricone family.)

Artist and author Leo Politi wrote and illustrated some 20 children's books, including *Bunker Hill, Pedro, the Angel of Olvera Street*, and *Song of the Swallows*, for which he won the Caldecott Medal. Philosophically and artistically avant-garde, his soothing watercolors and oil paintings celebrated cultural diversity and the spontaneity of children. Politi's mural, *The Blessing of the Animals*, graces the facade of the Biscailuz Building at El Pueblo Historical Monument. The artist's studio was once located on Olvera Street, where Politi could be found daily, painting mothers, children, and the other sights he held to be the essence of life. (Author's collection.)

Organized in 1947 by Louis J. Canepa as its
first president, the umbrella organization
Federated Italo Americans encompasses over
70 Southern California Italian organizations.
Its annual activities, including Columbus
Day and Republic Day, play a significant
role in the sustenance of Italian culture in
Los Angeles. (Courtesy of Mario Trecco.)

Los Angeles Superior Court judge Mario
Clinco (right) and attorneys Michael
Angelo Pontrelli, August "Gene" Carloni,
Paul Caruso, Eugene Damiano, and
Tony Capozolla founded the Italian
American Lawyers Association in 1977.
It is considered among the most dynamic
bar associations in Southern California.

123

Formed as a mutual aid society in New York City in 1905, Order of Sons of Italy in America is the nation's largest and oldest organization for men and women of Italian heritage. The Sons of Italy Hollywood Chapter, following tradition that spans over a century, promotes Italian culture and supports a multitude of philanthropic causes. (Courtesy of the Sons of Italy Hollywood.)

In 2002, community leaders organized the first annual Feast of San Gennaro Los Angeles. Similar to the New York City tradition, the Hollywood feast celebrates Italian culture, food, and entertainment and features live music, street performers, a procession, children's activities, and amusements. (Courtesy of the Sons of Italy Hollywood.)

The Los Angeles City Council proclaimed October "Italian Month" in the City of Los Angeles in 2007. Since then, community leaders have organized a series of cultural, social, and educational activities to celebrate the contributions of Italians to the city. Pictured from left to right are Los Angeles councilman Dennis P. Zine, Federated Italo Americans president Nicola D'Egidio, Ronnie Marmo, Mariann Gatto, Historic Italian Hall Foundation president Josephine Mahoney, councilman Eric Garcetti, councilman José Huizar, Italian Consul General Nicola Faganello, Carmela Funicello, councilman Tom LaBonge, councilwoman Janice Hahn, National Italian American Foundation's Marcella Leonetti Tyler, councilman Bill Rosendahl, Joe Cerrell, and Christine Giuliano. (Author's collection.)

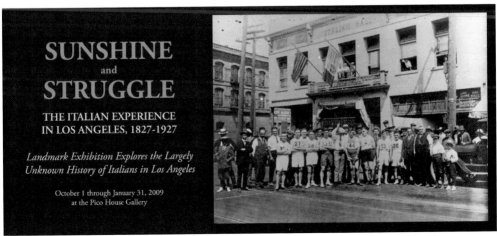

In 2008, the Historic Italian Hall Foundation, in collaboration with El Pueblo Historical Monument, produced a landmark exhibition entitled Sunshine and Struggle: The Italian Experience in Los Angeles. (Courtesy of the Historic Italian Hall Foundation.)

Hundreds of people attended the exhibit's opening reception, where they shared memories and discovered a seldom examined chapter in the city's history. (Courtesy of Joseph Gatto.)

The exhibit, which was the first of its kind in Los Angeles, featured never-before-seen photographs of the city's Italian enclave, artifacts, and interpretive displays, such as a c. 1900 Italian grocery store. For many Italians, the glance of their past inspired a keener vision of their future in the City of Angels. (Courtesy of Joseph Gatto.)